✒ RELIGION AND THE FOUNDING OF THE AMERICAN REPUBLIC

RELIGION AND THE FOUNDING OF THE AMERICAN REPUBLIC

 JAMES H. HUTSON

WITH A FOREWORD BY JAROSLAV PELIKAN *Yale University*

1998   LIBRARY OF CONGRESS   *Washington*

Distributed by University Press of New England   Hanover and London

Development and publication of this book was made possible by a generous gift from Mr. and Mrs. Henry J. (Bud) Smith and The Pew Charitable Trusts. The exhibition was made possible by grants from Mr. and Mrs. Henry J. (Bud) Smith, The Pew Charitable Trusts, and the Lilly Endowment Inc.

⊗ *The paper in this publication meets the requirements for permanence established by the American National Standard ANSI/NISO 239.48.1992. Permanence of Paper for Publications and Documents in Libraries and Archives.*

Library of Congress Cataloguing-in-Publication Data

Hutson, James H.

  Religion and the founding of the American Republic / by James H. Hutson ; with a foreword by Jaroslav Pelikan.

    p. cm.

  Includes bibliographical references and index.

  ISBN 0-8444-0948-0 (alk. paper)

---- ------ *Z6634.15*

  1. Church and state—United States. 2. Church and state—United States—Exhibitions. 3. United States—Church history—To 1775. 4. United States—Church history—To 1775—Exhibitions. 5. United States—Church history—18th century. 6. United States—Church history—18th century—Exhibitions. 7. United States—Church history—19th century. 8. United States—Church history—19th century—Exhibitions. 9. Religion and culture— United States—Exhibitions. 10. Library of Congress—Exhibitions. I. Title.

BR516.H785 1998   *97-45620*

322'.1'0973074753—dc21   *CIP*

Design: Adrianne Onderdonk Dudden

The Tree of Life. **Hand-colored engraving, printed for John Hagerty, Baltimore, 1791. Maryland Historical Society, Baltimore, Maryland.**

John Hagerty (b. 1747) was a Methodist preacher who established himself as a printer-publisher in Baltimore in the 1790s, where he specialized in printing evangelical works, including a biography of John Wesley. In addition to the Tree of Life, *Hagerty in 1791 published prints depicting a* Tree of Virtues *and a* Tree of Vices, *motifs used in religious art for centuries. The* Tree of Life, *based on Revelations 22:2, brings forth, under the redemptive rays of God as Father, Spirit, and Word, twelve fruits of salvation for those who seek entry into the New Jerusalem. A large crowd of their brethren are seen complacently strolling along the Broad Way to the Bottomless Pit, where the Devil and "Babylon Mother of Harlots" beckon. The secure sinners are stigmatized with the following labels: "pride," "chambering & wantonness," "quack," "usury," and "extortion."*

CONTENTS ⚘

FOREWORD ✢

The spirit of a people often finds a more profound and lasting expression in its hymns and anthems, whether official or unofficial, than it does in its constitutions and laws. The official national anthem of the United States, "The Star-Spangled Banner," affirms:

> Then conquer we must, for our cause it is
>   just—
> And this be our motto, "In God is our trust!"

In its unofficial anthems that affirmation is, if anything, intensified, as in Samuel Francis Smith's "America" (to the tune, let it be remembered, of "God Save the King!"):

> Long may our land be bright
> With freedom's holy light;
> Protect us by thy might,
>   Great God, *our* King!

And with overtly Christian tones in Julia Ward Howe's "Battle-Hymn of the Republic."

> In the beauty of the lilies Christ was born across
>   the sea,
> With a glory in his bosom that transfigures you
> and me,

As he died to make men holy, let us die to
make men free,
While God is marching on.

And, perhaps most transcendently of all, with echoes both from the Book of Revelation and from Augustine's *City of God*, in "America the Beautiful":

> O beautiful for patriot dream
>   That sees beyond the years
> Thine alabaster cities gleam
>   Undimmed by human tears!

In each case, significantly, the credo comes in the closing stanza of the anthem; only the "Battle-Hymn of the Republic" keeps up the apocalyptic tone from beginning to end. But each poem expresses something special about the American faith experience: "In God is our trust"; "Great God, our King"; "While God is marching on"; "Thine alabaster cities gleam."

How was it possible for this tradition to coexist with what later generations have somewhat simplistically interpreted to be the Jeffersonian tradition of an absolute "wall of separation" between church and state? That is the intriguing historical question to which the fascinating assemblage of materials in this exhibition and the remarkable narrative in this companion volume by Dr. James Hutson are addressed, showing that, both in theory and especially in practice, the separation was, from the beginning, anything but "absolute." Any answer to the question, therefore, must be not only far more complex than recent ideology has imagined, but also more subtle and nuanced than many historians have supposed. Nevertheless, several components for an answer do arise from this history. Taken together, these pictures and texts will be especially helpful to those who, like myself, are not primarily specialists in American history.

Skillfully picking his way through the minefield of conflicting claims about which religious tradition may take credit for American democracy, Dr. Hutson examines the diverse political philosophies at work in each of them and assesses the bearing of these philosophies on the Revolution and the Constitution. One of the strengths of the book is its balance of attention between popular religion and the official pronouncements of churchmen and politicians, with some quotable quotes from both sources. That balance is born out in the exhibition as well, which displays scrimshaw and other folk art alongside architecture, both vernacular and monumental, philosophical and theological treatises, and Thomas Jefferson's handwritten copy of the Lord's Prayer.

The tendency in much of the scholarly literature on this controverted topic has been to concentrate on the church groups in colonial America with a British connection, Anglicans and various kinds of Dissenters, including Pennsylvania Quakers and Boston Unitarians. The denominational provenance of the signers of the Declaration of Independence and the Constitution amply justifies such a concentration. But this narrative recognizes that it is important to pay attention also to other communities, both Christian and Jewish, some of which would become increasingly prominent in the nineteenth and twentieth centuries, as what one part of the exhibition calls "Republican Religion" developed still further.

It is characteristic of a "Whig interpretation of history" to imagine that history could not have come out any differently from the way it did, and, in the history of science or the history of ideas, for example, to chart the steps leading to that outcome, at the cost of the welter of other possibilities that were at work. The chapter entitled "Religion and the Congress of the Confederation, 1774–89," therefore, is especially valuable; for it documents again the highly experimental atmosphere out of which the Constitution, and then the Bill of Rights, would finally emerge. There was not one single paradigm of church and state going into the Congress of the Confederation in 1774—nor one single paradigm coming out of it fifteen years later. And the alternative possibilities that surfaced during the debates all went on to have a life of their own during the two centuries that followed, as they still do, even as we speak.

Because of the First Amendment of the American Constitution, many histories of religion in America shift focus at midpoint, from church-state relations in each of the several colonies during the seventeenth and eighteenth centuries to the federal treatment of church-state relations in the new American Republic after that. But the First Amendment specifically legislated what the *Federal Congress* could and could not do, reserving to the several states the right to order church-state relations after their own fashion; only with the Fourteenth Amendment were its provisions extended to the states. Even to someone who knows, for example, how long Congregationalism remained established in Connecticut, it is an eye-opener to read the chapter on "Religion and the State Governments."

Sometimes more implicit than explicit, but nevertheless evident from where we stand now, is the capacity of this outlook of the Framers to include within its affirmations and aspirations entire populations that could not participate in the original events. Speaking now as the son of immigrants from Slavic Europe who did not come to the United States until the beginning of the present century, I recall, with a mixture of amusement and resentment, how "different" and excluded I felt when the textbooks of my elementary schools spoke about "*our* Pilgrim forefathers" (no "foremothers" in those days!) and even about the threats to "*our* American way of life" that came from the new arrivals swarming into America out of Eastern and Central Europe—such as my grandparents and parents! Similar resentment—but eventually, I hope, also similar amusement—is an appropriate response from all those others whose ethnic tradition and religious faith make them somehow "different," too. But it is testimony to the abiding power of the evidence that comes from this exhibition and this history that these words and objects point beyond themselves, beyond the particularities of their own backgrounds to a universality of "e pluribus unum," with which each community has found it possible—and, please God, may still find it possible—to identify.

Jaroslav Pelikan
Sterling Professor Emeritus, Yale University
Immediate Past President,
The American Academy of Arts and Sciences

PREFACE ⚭

This volume has been prepared as a companion piece for the Library of Congress exhibition, *Religion and the Founding of the American Republic*, which opens in the Library's Thomas Jefferson Building, June 4, 1998. James H. Hutson, the author of this volume, is also the curator of the exhibition, the Chief of the Library's Manuscript Division, and a distinguished scholar of early American history.

The wide variety of materials in the superb collections of the Library of Congress creates a unique national resource for mounting an exhibit on religion and the founding of the United States. The Library's Manuscript Division holds the major collections of the papers of Thomas Jefferson and James Madison, the Founders most instrumental in establishing the church-state policy of the new nation, as well as the papers of many of their colleagues who also interested themselves in this issue—George Washington and Benjamin Franklin, for example. The Library's Rare Book and Special Collections Division contains thousands of pamphlets and broadsides covering all aspects of religion in early America. The iconography of early American religion can be seen in the collections of the Prints and Photographs Division; its sounds can

be heard in the revival hymnals and psalm books held in the Music Division.

Like most exhibits at the Library of Congress, this one seeks largely to share with a broad audience interesting material in the Library's collections. The religious aspects of American history do not seem to have been the central subject matter of major exhibitions in large public institutions in recent years. Because of this general neglect, the historical importance of this particular subject, and the careful and balanced scholarship of Dr. Hutson, this volume should make an important contribution to broad public knowledge as well as provide valuable reading for viewers of the exhibition.

The exhibition (and the companion volume) are not intended to provide a comprehensive history of religion on the North American continent from the seventeenth to the nineteenth centuries. The exhibition focuses on the relation of religion to government during the Founding period and does not cover other significant subjects in the broader field of early American religion, such as the religious practices of Native Americans or religion in Spanish and French North America. In planning the exhibition, it became apparent that justice could not be done to these and a number of other rich subjects in the context of a show focusing on church-state relations in the early republic.

The exhibition extends into the 1830s in order to follow the fortunes of evangelicalism, which appeared with great force on the American landscape in the 1730s and 1740s and became the dominant feature of American religion in the first three decades of the nineteenth century. By telling the story of evangelicalism through the 1830s, the exhibit is able to include distinctive American denominations that evangelicalism fostered, such as the African Methodist Episcopal Church and the Disciples of Christ—and also to trace the emergence in the 1820s and 1830s of the Church of Jesus Christ of Latter-Day Saints.

The overall picture that emerges from the exhibition will not surprise students of the Founding period. George Washington proclaimed in his Farewell Address in 1796 that religion, as the source of morality, was "a necessary spring of popular government." Tocqueville observed in 1835 in *Democracy in America* that Americans believed religion to be "indispensable to the maintenance of republican government," and to the flourishing of the unique civil society that—somewhat to his surprise—was making democracy work in a large country. How, or if, religion was to be encouraged by the state and whether the health of religion was to be left entirely to private endeavors were difficult questions which confronted the Founders, and which the present exhibition seeks to explore.

Viewers may be surprised by the evidence presented in the exhibition of the extent to which federal facilities were placed at the disposal of religion after the Founders moved the government to Washington in 1800. Based on extensive research, the curator has stated, with what appears to be ample justification, that on Sundays during the first years in Washington "the state became the church." Perhaps more surprising still is the enthusiasm with which Thomas Jefferson supported this development. There are still other fresh interpretations and little known materials in the exhibition which ought to stimulate wide interest.

The Library deeply appreciates the grants from Mr. and Mrs. Henry J. (Bud) Smith of Dallas, Texas, and The Pew Charitable Trusts of Philadelphia, Pennsylvania, that have made this volume possible; from Mr. Smith, The Pew Charitable Trusts and the Lilly Endowment Inc., of Indianapolis, Indiana, that have supported the exhibition; and from the Lilly Endowment Inc. for supporting the national tour of the exhibition.

James H. Billington
The Librarian of Congress

ACKNOWLEDGMENTS

It was a great pleasure working with my editor, Sara Day, whose skills and energy are extraordinary and whose insights contributed immeasurably to this book. She was assisted in the gathering of illustrations from lending institutions by Nawal Kawar and Gloria Baskerville-Holmes, also of the Publishing Office. My colleague, Staley Hitchcock, was a constant source of support. The members of the Advisory Committee collectively and individually gave me far more assistance than I had any right to expect. They are: Professor Patricia Bonomi, New York University; Professor Thomas Buckley, S.J., Jesuit School of Theology at Berkeley; Professor Richard Bushman, Columbia University; Dr. Michael Crawford, Head, Early History Branch, Naval Historical Center; Professor Daniel Dreisbach, American University; Professor Nathan Hatch, Notre Dame University; Professor Mark Noll, Wheaton College; Dr. Michael Novak, American Enterprise Institute; and Professor James Smylie, Union Theological Seminary.

Many people throughout the country have assisted me in planning and organizing the exhibition. I would like to give special thanks to the following, to whom I have turned on numerous occasions and who have been unfailingly helpful: Fred Anderson, Director, Virginia Baptist Historical Society; George M. Barringer, Director of Special Collections, Georgetown University Library; B. Schlessinger Ross, Executive Director, Society of Friends of Touro Synagogue; Ken Ross, Presbyterian Historical Society, Philadelphia; the Reverend Edwin Schell, Director, Lovely Lane Museum, Baltimore; Robert Schoeberlein, Curator, Prints and Photographs, Maryland Historical Society; Margaret Shannon, Curator of Rare Books, Washington National Cathedral; and the Reverend James Trimble, Rector, Christ Church, Philadelphia.

The staff members of the Library's Interpretive Programs Office, who mounted this exhibition with their customary skill, are: Irene Chambers, Interpretive Programs Officer; Giulia Adelfio, Exhibit Director; Debbie Durbeck; Chris O'Connor; Tambra Johnson; Gwynn Wilhelm; Denise Agee; and, from the Conservation Office, Rikki Condon. The assistance of the Development Office staff, particularly Norma Baker, Director of Development, and Jan Lauridsen was invaluable.

James H. Hutson

CHRONOLOGY ✧

1607	Virginia founded. Church of England planted in British North America.
1620	Plymouth settled by Pilgrims.
1629–30	Massachusetts Bay Colony founded. Congregationalism planted in British North America.
1634	Maryland founded. Roman Catholic Church planted in British North America.
1636	Roger Williams expelled from Massachusetts. He founds Rhode Island as a haven for religious dissidents.
1654	Jews, fleeing religious persecution in Brazil, arrive in New York City.
1659–62	Quakers hanged in Massachusetts, persecuted in Virginia; victims of the prevailing belief in enforced religious uniformity.
1681	William Penn, leader of the Quakers, receives a charter for Pennsylvania; Penn establishes religious liberty in the colony.
1683	Members of German sects begin arriving in Pennsylvania, attracted by religious liberty.
1689	English Parliament passes the Toleration Act which improves the conditions of dissenters throughout the American colonies.
ca. **1735–45**	The Great Awakening, a religious revival throughout the English-speaking world, invigorates and polarizes religious life in America.
1755	Separate Baptists, a product of the Great Awakening, begin proselytizing in the South.
1758	Presbyterian Church, split by the Great Awakening into New Side and Old Side, reunites.
1766	First Methodist meeting (in New York City) in the American colonies.

1776	American independence declared.
1780	Massachusetts Constitution adopted; state support of religion provided.
1784	Methodist Episcopal Church established.
1786	Jefferson's Bill for Establishing Religious Freedom passed by Virginia Assembly; state support of religion prohibited.
1787	U.S. Constitution adopted; religious tests for public service under the federal government prohibited.
1788–89	Protestant Episcopal Church established; ties with Church of England cut; Presbyterian Church also established on a new footing.
1789	Bill of Rights passed by Congress; proscribes congressional "establishment" of religion and congressional interference with the "free exercise thereof."
1800	Major revivals in Kentucky which spread east and initiate a long period of evangelical dominance in American religion.
1816	African Methodist Episcopal Church established.
1830	Joseph Smith founds Church of Jesus Christ of Latter-Day Saints (Mormons).
1832	Disciples of Christ established.
1833	Massachusetts becomes the final jurisdiction to renounce state support of religion.
1835	Tocqueville's *Democracy in America* published, in which the famous French commentator observed that Americans considered religion "indispensable to the maintenance of republican institutions."

RELIGION AND THE FOUNDING OF THE AMERICAN REPUBLIC

EUROPEAN PERSECUTION   *Many who settled British North America were driven to the New World by religious persecution, conducted by European states seeking to secure religious uniformity in their dominions. Uniformity was sought by Catholic and Protestant countries alike (and, in the seventeenth century, by Virginia and New England), with the result that the faith that controlled political power persecuted dissenters. In the name of Jesus Christ, Catholics killed Protestants and Protestants killed Catholics; both groups harassed and killed dissenting coreligionists. Religious persecution, as observers in every century have noted, has a fearful tendency to be sanguinary and implacable.*

Murder of David van der Leyen and Levina Ghyselins, Ghent, 1554. Engraving by J. Luyken, from T. J. V. Bracht (or Thieleman van Braght), *Het Bloedig Touneel de Martelaers Spiegel.* . . . (Amsterdam, 1685). Rare Book and Special Collections Division (LC-USZ62-119890).

Van der Leyen and Ghyselins were Dutch Anabaptists—some have described them as Mennonites—killed by Catholic authorities in 1554. Strangled and burned, van der Leyen was dispatched with an iron fork when signs of life were still detected in him. Bracht's Martyrs' Mirror is considered by modern Mennonites as second only in importance to the Bible in perpetuating their faith.

ONE ❦

AMERICA AS A RELIGIOUS REFUGE:
THE FOUNDING OF THE BRITISH NORTH AMERICAN COLONIES IN THE SEVENTEENTH CENTURY

Many of the people who settled British North America in the seventeenth century came for religious reasons, for the opportunity to worship God in ways that were unacceptable in Europe. Their passion for their faith was transmitted to their descendants who created the American nation in 1776. This legacy of faith, periodically refashioned and refreshed, gave to the new country the strong religious flavor that, in the nineteenth century, impressed foreign and domestic observers and, in 1922, prompted G. K. Chesterton (1874–1936), with ample justification, to call the United States "a nation with the soul of a church."[1]

For the men and women of faith who crossed the Atlantic in the seventeenth century, America was, in John Winthrop's words, a religious "refuge." Seventeenth-century Europe was full of religious fervor and hatred because it had not yet come to terms with the Protestant Reformation of the preceding century. Both Catholics and Protestants believed that there was a true religion, that they had it, and that others, in their own interest, should be compelled to conform to it, lest, deluded by false doctrine, they lose their souls. To impose religious uniformity, seventeenth-century Europeans tortured, maimed, and murdered individuals, fought wars, and displaced populations.

England did not escape these plagues. After Elizabeth I (1533–1603) imposed a religious settlement in 1559, Catholics were considered potential traitors. Protestants, on whose behalf the Queen acted, began quarreling with each other. Those who wanted to continue cleansing the Church of England of residues of Roman Catholicism were called Puritans. There was no consensus among the Puritans about how far reforms should go. A small minority believed that the Anglican Church was so corrupt that they must withdraw immediately to seek the Lord while He might still be found. Taking as their motto a pamphlet, *Reformation without Tarrying for any*, they hastened to Holland. From there they sailed to Plymouth, Massachusetts, in 1620.[2] These were, of course, the Pilgrims whose courage, suffering, and piety were celebrated by later generations of American historians far out of proportion to their mini-

3

Execution and mutilation of John Ogilvie (Ogilby), S. J., Glasgow, Scotland, March 10, 1615. Engraving from Mathias Tanner, *Societas Jesu usque ad Sanguinis et vitae profusionem Militans . . .* (Prague, 1675). Rare Book and Special Collections Division (LC-USZ62-119891).

Jesuits like John Ogilvie (Ogilby) (1580–1615), who was sentenced to death by a Glasgow court in the winter of 1615, were under constant surveillance and in constant danger under the Protestant governments of England and Scotland.

mal influence on the nation's development. For the Pilgrims, it was enough to live quietly in a corner of Massachusetts in "sweet communion" with God.

The great majority of Puritans rejected headlong separation from the Church of England and sought instead to reform it from within. Their hopes were dashed in the late 1620s when the leadership of the church, backed by the civil authorities, insisted that they adopt religious ceremonies and practices that they abhorred. Puritan ministers who refused to conform were fired from their pulpits and threatened with "extirpation from the earth" unless they and their followers toed the line.[3] Exemplary punishments were inflicted on Puritan stalwarts;

one zealot, for example, who called Anglican bishops "knobs, wens and bunchy popish flesh," was sentenced, in 1630, to life imprisonment, had his property confiscated, his nose slit, an ear cut off, and his forehead branded S.S. (sower of sedition).[4] Far from being cowed by these barbarities, the future emigrants to America were one in spirit with the woman who exclaimed, at the mutilation of another Puritan leader, that "there are many hundreds which by God's assistance would willingly suffer for the cause you suffer for this day."[5]

There were, however, alternatives to martyrdom. One that became increasingly attractive was migration to the New World. As many as twenty

Lutheran religious refugees, fleeing Salzburg, Austria.
Frontispiece engraving from [Christopher Sancke ?], *Ausführliche Historie derer Emigranten oder*
Vertriebenen Lutheraner aus dem Erz-Bistum Salzburg **(Leipzig, 1732).**
Rare Book and Special Collections Division (LC-USZ62-119892).

On October 31, 1731, Catholic Archbishop Leopold von Firmian issued an edict expelling as many as twenty thou-
sand Lutherans from his principality of Salzburg, Austria. After a stay in London, some of the refugees settled in
Georgia; others went to the Netherlands or to East Prussia. The man has under one arm a copy of the Augsburg
Confession and under the other a theological work by Johann Arndt (1555–1621); the woman is carrying the
Bible. The legend between them says: "we are driven into exile for the Gospel's sake; we leave our homeland and are
now in God's hands." At the top is a Scriptural verse, Matthew 24:20: "but pray that your flight does not occur in
the winter or on the Sabbath."

**Cottonus Matherus [Cotton Mather], 1727.
Mezzotint by Peter Pelham, 1728 (Restrike, 1860).
Prints and Photographs Division (LC-USZC4-4597).**

*Cotton Mather (1663–1728), the best-known New England
Puritan divine of his generation, was a controversial figure in his
own time and remains so among scholars today. A formidable
intellect and a prodigious writer—he published some 450 books
and pamphlets—Mather was at the center of all of the major
political, theological, and scientific controversies of his era.
A courageous advocate of inoculation for smallpox, Mather has
been accused, unfairly, of instigating the Salem witchcraft trials.*

**Cotton Mather, draft fragments of a sermon.
Miscellaneous Manuscript Collection,
Manuscript Division (LCMS-39956-163).**

A draft, not further identified, of one of Cotton Mather's sermons.

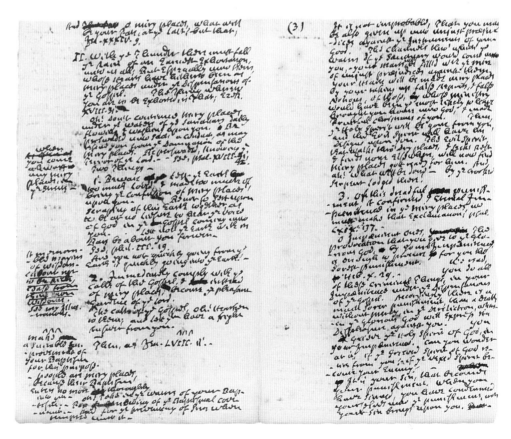

thousand Puritans, it has been estimated, poured out of England by 1642, the majority congregating in New England, others spreading as far south as the West Indies. These were people who had walked miles on empty stomachs in England to hear the gospel preached with truth and power and who forsook their "dearest relations, Parents, brethren, Sisters, Christian friends, and acquaintances, overlook[ed] all the dangers and difficulties of the vast Seas, the thought wereof was a terrour to many, and all this to go to a wildernesse . . . onely in hopes of enjoying Christ in his Ordinances."[6] The purpose of the Puritans was described by John Winthrop (1588–1647) aboard ship heading for Massachusetts in 1630 in words so striking that they have become a slogan for modern politicians; "wee shall be as a Citty upon a Hill," said Winthrop; "wee are Commaunded this day to loue the Lord our God, and to loue one another to walke in his wayes and to keepe his Commaundements and his Ordinance and his lawes . . . that wee may liue and be multiplyed, and that the Lord our God may blesse vs in the land whether wee goe to possesse it."[7]

Once in New England the Puritans organized themselves top to bottom to create the kind of society they believed the Scriptures required. The church was constructed on the Congregational model—independent, covenanted groups of men and women who could publicly prove that they had been saved—a model that many hoped the people of England would imitate as soon as they saw it up and running in the New World. In so far as possible, laws were based on the Bible. Magistrates, in the Reformed tradition, were exalted as "public ministers of God." They were expected to—and did—use the full power of the state to promote the agenda of the church. Taking stock of their achievements in 1643, the Puritans declared that "all came

into these parts of America with one and the same end, namely, to advance the kingdom of our Lord Jesus Christ, and to enjoy the liberties of the gospel in purity with peace."[8] New England was a "plantation of religion" and proud of it.[9]

Today some of the things the Puritans said and did seem ugly. Although they were committed to converting the native populations to Christianity, they did not respect their new neighbors and said so. The Puritans and other seventeenth-century English settlers, the Quakers excepted, routinely called the Indians savages, heathens, and infidels, terms that sound like racial slurs to the twentieth-century ear. This attitude, whether in New England or Virginia, did not promote conversion, although some Puritan ministers distinguished themselves by the vigor with which they sought to bring the Indians to Christ. John Eliot (1604–1690), for example, translated the Bible into the native tongue and at one point ministered to eleven hundred "Praying Indians," organized into fourteen New England-style towns.

The Puritans' views on dissent repel twentieth-century Americans. They did not believe in permitting differences of opinion in religion. The "business" of the first settlers, a Puritan minister recalled in 1681, "was not Toleration, but [they] were professed Enemies of it."[10] The Puritans subscribed to the view that informed nearly every contemporary European government, that civil authorities must assist the church in maintaining religious uniformity. The Puritans had no quarrel with the English government's policy, under which they suffered, of imposing on the realm one true religion; they disagreed only over what one religion was true. In control in New England, the Puritans relentlessly suppressed dissent; "the very neck of Schism and vile opinions," they boasted, "was broken" in the Bible

Commonwealth.[11] Those "venomous weeds," the Quakers, were expelled from Massachusetts and four were hanged between 1659 and 1661, when they defiantly returned.[12] Presbyterians and Baptists were banished. Some of the Puritans' choicest spirits, such as Roger Williams (1603–1683), were driven out when they would not retract controversial opinions.

Ejected from Massachusetts in the winter of 1636, Williams founded Rhode Island as a "shelter for persons distressed for conscience," as a refuge outside the larger Puritan refuge for men and women seeking to live where government would not interfere with religious beliefs and practices.[13] A collection of what conventional Puritans regarded as religious oddballs followed Williams to Rhode Island—"the latrina of New England,"[14] in the orthodox view—but the new colony protected even those whom Williams regarded as dangerously misguided, for nothing could change his view that "forced worship stinks in God's nostrils."[15]

Among those who sought sanctuary in Rhode Island was America's first major female religious figure, Anne Hutchinson (1591–1643). Upon arriving in Massachusetts in 1634, Mrs. Hutchinson, a brilliant, energetic woman, began operating as a kind of freelance theologian, tackling the most abstruse problems of Puritan theology and explaining them in ways that appealed to many ordinary people but offended most of the ministers and their political allies. Fearing that her activities, if unchecked, would convulse the colony, the magistrates of Massachusetts brought her to trial under conditions that reflected little credit on Puritan justice and banished her from Boston in 1638.

By 1658, Jews, objects of perennial persecution, came to Rhode Island to enjoy religious liberty. They had been preceded in North America four years earlier by a group of twenty-three brethren who landed in New Amsterdam, fleeing a possible pogrom in Brazil. For some decades Jews had flourished in Dutch-held areas of Brazil, but a Portuguese conquest of the area in 1654 confronted them with the prospect of the introduction of the Inquisition which had recently (1647) burned a Brazilian Jew at the stake. A shipload of Jewish refugees from Dutch Brazil, their original destination unknown, landed in New Amsterdam in the fall of 1654 and threw themselves on the mercy of the community, which helped them survive the winter. The Dutch governor, the pompous Peter Stuyvesant (1592–1672), lacked Roger Williams' generosity of spirit and tried to make it difficult for the Jews to practice their religion, but regular services were established in 1655. British conquest of New Amsterdam in 1664 improved the lot of the Jews and by the late colonial period small numbers were thriving in various colonial seaports.[16]

South of New York, Pennsylvania was settled by Quakers, who shared with the Puritans of New England the ambitious hope that their "Holy Experiment" would be "an example . . . Sett up to the nations."[17] The Quakers, or Religious Society of Friends (as they preferred to be called), coalesced in England in 1652 around a charismatic leader, George Fox (1624–1691). Today many scholars regard them as radical Puritans, an identification that both groups would have loathed. This affiliation is credible, however, because the Quakers carried many Puritan convictions to extremes. They stretched the sober deportment of the Puritans into a glorification of "plainness." Theologically, they expanded the Puritan concept of a church of individuals regenerated by the Holy Spirit to the idea of the indwelling of the Spirit or the "Light of Christ" in every person. Salvation was available to anyone who would open himself or herself—Quakers scandalized their contemporaries by stressing the equal-

Sefardi Torah scroll, [eighteenth century ?]. Hebraic Section, African and Middle Eastern Division.

A Torah scroll contains the Five Books of Moses. Inscribed by hand "in good ink and with a fine pen" on a parchment prepared from the skin of a kosher animal, it is read in synagogues on the Sabbath, holidays, and at morning services on Mondays and Thursdays. The Torah scroll pictured here was prepared according to the Sephardic tradition, which was followed in American colonial synagogues and would have closely resembled those used in seventeenth- and eighteenth-century Jewish houses of worship.

ity of the sexes—to the power of God within. "The whole tendency of their preaching," wrote the famous Quaker apostate, George Keith (1638–1716) in 1702, "was that the Light within every Man was sufficient to his salvation without anything else."[18]

"Without anything else" is what got the Quak-ers into trouble with the authorities, for they believed that the Inner Light made most of organized religion irrelevant. The sacraments were considered to be unnecessary, as was a trained ministry. The Bible was not binding, for it was only "a declaration of the fountain, not the fountain itself."[19] To their contemporaries, the Quakers seemed to be

Philadelphia: Quäkerkirche. **Wood engraving from Ernst von Hesse Wartegg,** *Nord-Amerika, seine Stadt und Naturwunder, das Land und seine Bewohner in Schilderung* **(Leipzig, 1888). General Collections (LC-USZ62-2511).**

This undated image depicts a feature of Quaker religious practice that made early Friends so repugnant to other denominations: their insistence on equality for women, including the right—in defiance of the apostle Paul's injunctions—to speak in meetings and to preach the Gospel.

scheming to purify Christianity out of existence. As a result, open season was declared on them in the press and in the courts. Typical of the literary tirades against them was John Brown's *Quakerisme the pathway to Paganisme* (1678), in which Quaker convictions were reviled as "the dreadfulest delusion of Satan, and of darkness, caused by the Prince of darkness, that ever was heard of in the Christian world." William Penn (1644–1718) was accused of being

a "greater AntiChrist than Julian the Apostate."[20]

Many thought that the Quakers deserved whatever physical violence they received. What if a Quaker received 117 lashes on the bare back; had not he and his companions "endeavoured to beat the Gospel ordinances black and blew?"[21] By 1680, ten thousand Quakers had been imprisoned in England and 243 had died from torture and mistreatment in the King's jails. This reign of terror impelled Friends to settle in New Jersey in the 1670s, where they were soon well entrenched. When William Penn in 1681 parlayed a debt owed by Charles II (1630–1685) to his father into a charter for the province of Pennsylvania, many more Quakers were prepared to grasp the opportunity to live in a land where they might worship freely. By 1685, as many as eight thousand Quakers had come to live in Pennsylvania.

It is often forgotten that the early Quakers were a proselytizing people, fired by a desire to convert their Christian neighbors. In 1703 an Anglican reported that their "missionaries do mightily swarme" from Virginia to Long Island. There is no doubt that the Friends invested more energy in spreading their message throughout the colonies than did the Puritans.[22] It is also indisputable that the Quakers were more eager to seek and suffer martyrdom than their northern neighbors. Whether this means that there was more religious zeal in seventeenth-century Pennsylvania than in New England is difficult to say. There was obviously no lack of it in either colony.

William Penn's most enduring contribution was the charter of government that he gave his fellow Quakers in 1682, specifically, his writing religious freedom into the law of the land. Penn understood religious freedom to be the severing of all connection between government and religious observances, although not between government and morality. In his famous *Frame of Government* (1682), Penn pledged that all citizens who believed in "One Almighty and Eternal God . . . shall in no wayes be molested or prejudiced for their religious Perswasion or Practice in matters of Faith and Worship, nor shall they be compelled at any time to frequent or maintain any Religious Worship, Place or Ministry whatever."[23] Penn did not minimize contemporary fears, which surfaced in 1776 in the new American state governments, that divorcing gov-

ernment from religion risked the creation of an immoral and possibly ungovernable citizenry. Declaring in the *Frame of Government* that "Wildness and Looseness of the People provoke the Indignation of God against a Country," Penn required his magistrates, whom he called in the Puritan fashion "ministers of God," to repress an encyclopedic list of moral offenses, including everything from "Prophane Talking" to "Whoredom" to "Stage Plays" and cock-fighting. Although Penn recognized that, in attempting to enforce morality, he was dealing with the "effect of evil" and not its cause, he was determined to use his full powers to keep Pennsylvanians a moral people and to prevent the extraordinary liberties he had provided from degenerating into licentiousness.

Roger Williams had anticipated Penn in separating the state from the church, but because of the size, location, and population of Pennsylvania—not for nothing was it called the Keystone State—the success of Penn and the Quakers in making religious freedom work made a much deeper impression on American and world history than Williams' efforts. Pennsylvania became, in fact, a point of reference a century later for Americans opposing plans for government-supported religion. "Witness the state of Pennsylvania," a group of Virginians urged its House of Delegates in 1785, "wherein no such [religious] Establishment hath taken place; their Government stands firm and which of the neighbouring States has better Members of brighter Morals and more upright Characters?"[24]

If Penn's promotion of religious liberty anticipated future American developments, so too did his creation of an ethnic melting pot in his new province. As soon as he received his charter, he began promoting Pennsylvania with a public relations campaign that flooded the European Continent with books and pamphlets in Dutch, German, and French. His target, initially, was sects sharing Quaker principles who had long been persecuted in Europe. Penn and his agents assured this audience that Pennsylvania offered "Liberty to all Peoples to worship God, according to their Faith and Persuasion."[25] Never one to underestimate the power of economic incentives, Penn also touted his province as a place to make a good living. He was comfortable mixing piety and the profit motive, believing with the early Jesuit leaders of Maryland that "while we sow spiritual seed we shall reap carnal things in abundance."[26]

Europe's oppressed Christians immediately responded to Penn's invitation, the first to come being a group of Mennonites (possibly including some Quakers) who arrived in Pennsylvania from Krefeld, Germany, in 1683. Their experience was typical of the German and Swiss sectarians who began flowing into Pennsylvania; they had been repeatedly banished from their homes and warned the last time, "if they come againe, they should be whipt and burnt on theire backs."[27] Swiss Mennonites, brutalized in Bern by being jailed and forced to work eighteen hours a day on bread and water, followed a few years later, and additional German groups—Dunkers, Schwenkfelders, and Moravians—arrived apace, with the result that, by the early eighteenth century, Pennsylvania came to resemble "an asylum for banished sects."[28]

Although a few sects engaged in outreach—the Moravians were particularly energetic in attempting to convert the native populations—most resembled the Pilgrims in seeking simply to go their own way. Some went way beyond the bounds of conventional religious practice. One group of Germans, led by a Rosicrucian, lived in caves along the banks of the Wissahickon Creek, awaiting the "Woman of the Wilderness," whose arrival would usher in the millennium;[29] another founded a utopian commune at Ephrata; still others met in houses and barns, practicing the primitive Christian rituals of footwashing and the Communion kiss, and baptizing their initiates by immersion, face down and to the east; another group of German Baptists was accused of trying to revive Judaism, by refusing to eat pork and circumcizing each other "after the Jewish manner."[30]

In the 1720s, Germans from the "mainline" Reformed and Lutheran churches began pouring into the province and numerically overwhelmed the sectarians who preceded them. The influence of the earlier groups persisted, however, because, in offering an alternative to their more conventional countrymen, they provided a form of competition that forced the mainline ministers constantly to brace up the convictions of their congregations. As the Germans spread west and then south into Virginia and the Carolinas, they carried with them their strong, if distinctive, religious faith. They also proved, as William Penn anticipated they would, that a profusion of religious views, many considered subversive in Europe, could coexist in a free land.

Immediately south of Pennsylvania, another group of Christians unwelcome in England—Roman Catholics—established yet another religious refuge in America. Driven by "the sacred duty of finding a refuge for his Roman Catholic brethren," George Calvert (1580–1632), a principal lieutenant of James I (1566–1625) until his religion cost him his job, obtained a charter from Charles I in 1632 for the territory between Pennsylvania and Virginia.[31] The Maryland charter offered no guidelines on religion, although it assumed that Catholics would not be molested in the new colony. A "General Toleration" was, in fact, established "by which all sorts

Pedilavium das Füsswaschen der Schwestern. **Engraving from David Cranz,** *Kurze, zuverlässige Nachricht, von der,* *unter den Namen der Böhmisch-Mährischen Brüder bekannt, Kirche Unitas fratrum* **(Halle, 1757).** **The Library Company of Philadelphia.**

Many of the German sects, which began emigrating to Pennsylvania in the late seventeenth and early eighteenth century, brought with them "primitive" Christian practices such as footwashing, seen here being conducted by the women of the Moravian Brethren.

who profess Christianity . . . might be at Liberty to worship God in such manner as was most agreeable with their respective Judgments and Consciences."³²

In 1634, two ships, the *Ark* and the *Dove*, brought the first settlers to Maryland. Aboard the vessels were approximately two hundred people, most of whom appear to have been Protestant servants. Among the passengers were two Catholic

priests who had been forced to board surreptitiously to escape the reach of English anti-Catholic laws. Upon landing in Maryland, the Catholics were transported by a profound reverence similar to that experienced by John Winthrop and the Puritans when they set foot in New England. The "Apostle to Maryland," Father Andrew White (1579–1656), described the celebration of the first

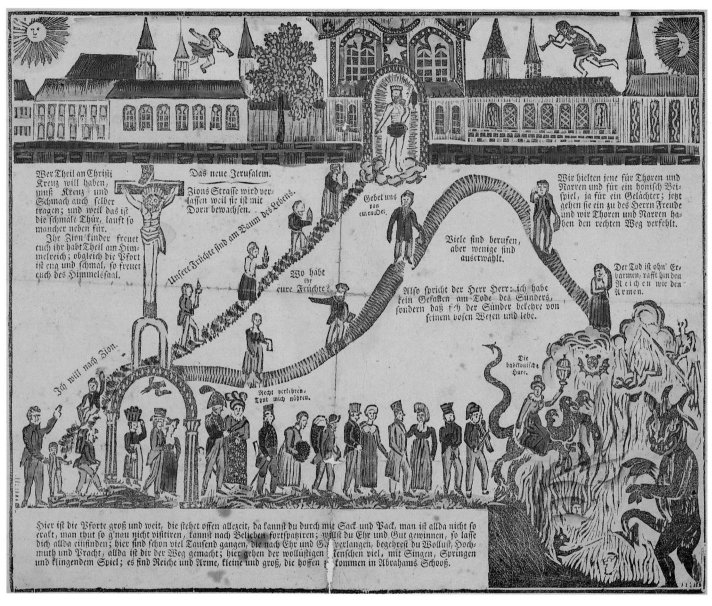

Das neue Jerusalem. Woodcut with watercolor, artist unidentified, early nineteenth century.
German Fraktur Collection, Prints and Photographs Division (LC–USZC4–4570).

A Pennsylvania German illustration uses a familiar nineteenth-century evangelical motif of the narrow gate to Heaven and the broad and seductive road to Hell, where the Devil and his minions awaited the self-satisfied sinner.

mass: "We celebrated mass for the first time . . . This had never been done before in this part of the world. After we had completed the sacrifice, we took upon our shoulders a great cross which we had hewn out of a tree, and advancing in order to the appointed place . . . we erected a trophy to Christ the Savior, humbly reciting, on our bended knees, the Litanies of the Sacred Cross, with great emotion."[33]

Catholic worship thrived during the first decade in Maryland. The Jesuits rose to the challenge of converting the local Indians; Father White was eminently successful with the Piscataways, producing a dictionary and grammar of their language and translating devotional literature into the native tongue. In the 1640s, religious passions generated by the English Civil War engulfed the province. Maryland Protestants, assisted by coreligionists from Virginia, seized control and deported White and other Catholic leaders to England in chains. Having reestablished their authority, Catholics in the Maryland Assembly in 1649 passed a Toleration Act that was progressive for the time, even if it established the death penalty for anti-Trinitarian Christians. The act stipulated that no orthodox Christian "shall from henceforth bee any waies troubled, molested, or discountenanced, for, or in respect of his or her religion nor in the free exercise thereof."[34] This act failed to soothe the troubled spirits in the province. In 1654, Protestants in the Assembly repealed it and, the next year, having defeated the Catholics in battle, they outlawed the Roman Catholic religion, ravaged the Jesuits' estates, expelled all priests, and hanged several Catholics.

The conflict in Maryland in the 1640s and 1650s showed the difficulty of establishing freedom of conscience in an age of religious passion. Sponsors of the concept, the Catholics did not have the numerical strength to sustain it, for they were a minority in the 1640s and continued to decline as a percentage of the population, comprising only one in ten in 1669. How remarkable, then, that Pennsylvania was able to make religious freedom work, long after the Quakers, its original promoters, were eclipsed numerically by unsympathetic religious groups.

Catholic political fortunes in Maryland revived in 1660 after the restoration of Charles II, only to be extinguished by the Glorious Revolution of 1689, which led to the legal establishment of the Church of England and the imposition of English penal laws which deprived Catholics of the right to vote and to hold office. Until the American Revolution, Catholics in Maryland were dissenters in their own country, living at times under a state of siege, but keeping loyal to their convictions, a faithful remnant awaiting better times.

To include seventeenth-century Virginia in a survey of religion, especially to compare her to the colonies north of the Potomac, glowing with the intensity of men and women who crossed an ocean rather than compromise their faith, seems perverse. Virginia, after all, was the land of laid-back religion, the home of a pleasure-loving population who considered it boorish to bother too much about spiritual concerns and who mocked their northern neighbors as religious fanatics and crackpots. This image of religion in Virginia, a fixture in many textbooks, was promoted by colonial Virginians themselves. Writing about his countrymen early in the eighteenth century, William Byrd II (1674–1744) said, "like true Englishmen, they built a church that cost no more than Fifty Pounds and a tavern that cost Five Hundred,"[35] the latter place being the haunt of too many Virginia clergymen, who, according to a critic in 1656, "could babble in a

Cecil Calvert presenting to Lycurgus his
"Act Concerning Religion," 1649.
Engraving by James Barry, 1793.
Prints and Photographs Division
(photograph courtesy of Maryland
Historical Society, Baltimore, Maryland).

*In this fanciful depiction, Calvert is showing his Act
Concerning Religion to the ancient Spartan lawgiver,
Lycurgus. The act, which granted religious liberty to
trinitarian Christians, earned Calvert, in the artist's
opinion, a place in a long line of civil libertarians,
running, improbably, from the Saxon king, Alfred,
on Calvert's left through William Penn, looking
over Calvert's right shoulder, to Benjamin Franklin,
viewing the proceedings from Heaven in his familiar
fur hat.*

Pulpet, roare in a Tavern, exact from their Parishioners, and rather by their dissolutenesse destroy
than feed their Flocks."[36] Although there is a measure of truth in these descriptions, they substantially distort the condition of religion in the Old
Dominion.

Virginia was settled, not by the religious vision-
aries who were in command in the northern colonies, but by businessmen—operating through
a joint stock company, the Virginia Company of
London—who wanted to get rich. The colony

looked very different from its American neighbors.
Unlike New England and Pennsylvania, which were
settled by families, Virginia was populated by single
young men down on their luck, the homeless of
seventeenth-century London. The "very excre-
ments" of English society, these men died like flies
in the new colony.[37] Transportation to Virginia was
for them a persecution far more lethal than any
meted out to European religious dissidents. Like
William Penn and the Calverts, the entrepreneurs
running Virginia were frank about their desire to

make money. Nonetheless, they resembled the proprietors of Pennsylvania and Maryland in professing a concern for religion, conceiving themselves as "first and foremost Christians, and, above all, militant Protestants."[38] "Religion," according to an eminent authority on American colonial religion, "was the really energizing propulsion in this settlement, as in others."[39]

The businessmen of the Virginia Company kept their colony well supplied with ministers, more in proportion to the population than in England itself. The first ministers compared favorably to their better known brethren in the other colonies. The saintly Robert Hunt (1568–1608) impressed even Captain John Smith and presided over church services in every way as moving for their triumph over adversity as those in the other colonies. At first Hunt officiated under an "old saile," rigged up in the forest, his pulpit being a "bar of wood nailed to two neighboring trees." Later, Hunt preached in a "homely thing like a barne." He led "daily Common Prayer morning and evening" and preached twice on Sunday. After Hunt's death the colonists, on their own initiative, continued daily prayers and "a Homily on Sundaie" until replacement ministers arrived.[40] One of these was Alexander Whitaker (1585–1617), who established a ministry to the Indians—a goal written into the colony's first charter by James I—and conducted it with as much zeal as Eliot and White, his most famous convert being Pocahontas.

Lord Delaware (1577–1618), the governor who arrived in 1610, refurbished Hunt's barn-church with cedar and black walnut, built a steeple with two bells, and sweetened the sermons preached on Thursdays and Sundays with a constant supply of fresh flowers. Delaware was succeeded by a military man, Sir Thomas Dale (d. 1619), who acted

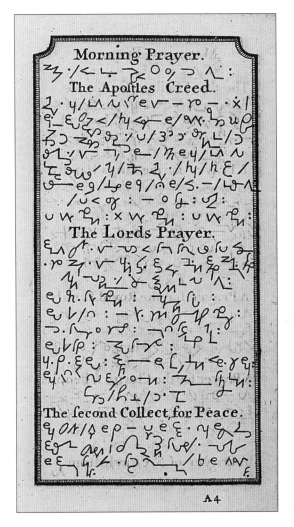

Morning Prayer. The Apostles Creed. The Lords Prayer. The Second Collect, for Peace from *The Book of Common Prayer in Short-Hand, According to Mr. Weston's Excellent Method. . . .* (London, 1730).
Rare Book and Special Collections Division.

In a preface to the prayer book, the creator of the shorthand system in which it was printed, James Weston, advised his readers that he had omitted the "Forms of Matrimony . . . at the Desire of the Subscribers, that the Price might be less."

like a crusader. Dale considered himself engaged in "religious warfare" and expected no reward "but from him in whose vineyard I labor, whose Church with greedy appetite I desire to erect."[41] Martial law was imposed on the colony and religion spread at the point of a sword. Everyone was required to attend church and be catechized by a minister. Those who refused could be executed or sent to the galleys. When a popular assembly, the House of Burgesses, was established in 1619, it enacted religious laws that were "a match for anything to be found in Puritan societies," strictly enjoining church attendance and Sabbath keeping.[42]

Although Virginia, during its first two decades, might not have looked like the New England settlements, it certainly sounded like them, for most of the ministers who came to the colony during its early years, whose views can be ascertained, were Puritans. They preached in the Puritan plain style and fed their flocks on Puritan doctrine. Like their brethren in New England they shared the view, common throughout Europe, that the state must impose one true religion in its jurisdiction. Accordingly, the Virginia House of Burgesses in 1632 passed a law requiring that there be a "uniformitie throughout this colony both in substance and circumstance to the cannons and constitutions of the Church of England. . . ."[43]

During the 1640s, as the church in Virginia became more self-consciously and aggressively Anglican, it welcomed the efforts of the civil authority to expel Puritan preachers in the name of religious uniformity. Beginning in 1659, Virginia enacted anti-Quaker laws as sweeping as any passed in New England, prescribing the death penalty for Friends who obstinately refused to keep away from the col-ony. In his *Notes on the State of Virginia* (1782), Thomas Jefferson (1743–1826) considered seventeenth-century Virginians in no way morally superior to the persecutors of the Quakers in Massachusetts: "if no capital execution took place here, as did in New-England, it was not," he wrote, "owing to the moderation of the church, or spirit of the legislature . . . but to historical circumstances which have not been handed down to us."[44]

The middle period of the seventeenth century was a time of trial and error for the Anglican Church in Virginia, as it came to terms with unprecedented problems, such as the size of parishes—some were sixty miles long. By the 1670s, a "significant reassertion of organized religious activity" was underway in the colony—a "renaissance," in the opinion of one expert.[45] Even earlier, in 1656, an observer, commenting on the loyalty of Virginians to their church, assured prospective ministers that "they would find an assisting, an embracing, a comforting people" in the Old Dominion.[46] At the end of the seventeenth century the church in Virginia, according to a recent authority, was prospering; it was "active and growing" and was "well attended by young and old alike."[47]

Virginia, then, was not the exception that proved the rule that religion reigned in seventeenth-century America. There were, to be sure, fewer people in the Old Dominion (and at points south), than in the northern colonies, for whom religion was the sole, consuming concern of their lives. But there were plenty of devout men and women south of the Potomac, and so many in the other colonies, that there can be no doubt—none whatsoever—that religion was the salt that flavored life in seventeenth-century British North America.

TWO ❧

RELIGION IN EIGHTEENTH-CENTURY AMERICA

For a long time, scholars argued that the salt of religion lost its savor in America after 1700. Religion, it was held, became cold and formal in the towns and all but disappeared along the expanding frontiers. The country's first major religious revival, the Great Awakening of the 1740s, is represented as giving Christianity a temporary boost, but, after the Awakening spent its force, religion is pictured as sinking back into a rut. By the time of the American Revolution, an indifferent population is seen as acquiescing in the program of leaders, nominally Christian, but committed to the agenda of the Enlightenment, who proceeded to send religion to the sidelines of American life.

This view is wrong, say recent authorities: according to one expert, religion in the eighteenth century was actually in the "ascension rather than the declension"; another sees a "rising vitality in religious life" from 1700 onward; a third goes even further and finds religion in many parts of the colonies in a state of "feverish growth."[1]

How did earlier scholars miss these positive trends in eighteenth-century religion? It appears that they were too credulous in accepting at face value pessimistic assessments of the colonial religious environment by clergymen, who inflated their own importance by picturing themselves as struggling to save a society that was settling into infidelity.

Reports of Anglican missionaries of the SPG (Society for the Propagation of the Gospel in Foreign Parts) have been particularly susceptible to misinterpretation. In dispatches to superiors in London, often swallowed whole by historians, these emissaries of the Church of England frequently claimed that America was a spiritual wasteland, overrun by "unruly Beasts" such as "St. Paul [had] to encounter." "Heathens and heretics," they continued, "superabound in these parts. Africa has not more monsters than America."[2] If the missionaries' reports are read in full, however, the truth emerges: the "monstrous heretics" of America were no more than zealous Quakers and Presbyterians, "stiff Dis-

Churches in eighteenth-century America came in all sizes and shapes, from plain, rough-hewn buildings in rural areas to elegant edifices in the cities. Compare the humble Baptist church in rural Virginia with its stately city cousin in Providence, Rhode Island, both built about the same time. Similar differences could be found in the churches of all denominations in eighteenth-century America.

ABOVE LEFT: **South Quay Baptist Church, Southampton County, Virginia.**
Virginia Baptist Historical Society, Richmond.

This church was founded in 1775, although it was not "formally organized" until ten years later.

ABOVE RIGHT: *A SW View of the Baptist Meeting House, Providence, R.I.*
Engraved by S. Hill for the *Massachusetts Magazine*, August 1789.
Prints and Photographs Division (LC-USZ62-31789).

Believed to be the first Baptist church in America, the Providence congregation was organized in 1639. The meeting house shown here was constructed in 1774–75 from plans by the architect John Brown, after a design by James Gibbs.

senters," whom the missionaries accused of poisoning the popular mind against the Church of England. The Anglican attitude was common in the eighteenth century: if not our religion, no religion.

European-bred ministers were also quick to charge Americans with another kind of religious defect: they had, it seemed, fallen prey to a "dangerous indifferentism." This complaint, when analyzed, was that Americans lacked concern, not for religion, but for the denominational distinctions that meant so much in Europe. They "do not imagine much real difference in Principle 'twixt Churchmen & Dissenters of all Denominations," fretted an Anglican minister in 1728.[3]

A more potent source of the notion that religion, after an inspired start, began floundering in colonial America was the rhetorical breastbeating of spokesmen for second and third generation Quakers and Puritans who considered themselves faithless stewards of their fathers' vineyards. These unhappy souls upbraided their fellow citizens for failing to sustain the religious intensity of the first generation and creating thereby an era of "declension" in religion. The Quakers were quite as good as the Puritans at self-flagellation. The descendants of William Penn, an eighteenth-century Quaker complained, had "suffered the plantation of God to be as a field uncultivated . . . [they] could not instruct their offspring in those statutes they had themselves forgotten."[4]

Puritan preachers of the 1660s and 1670s railed against the alleged backsliding of their generation. Uriah Oakes (1631–1681) charged in 1673 that his contemporaries were satisfied with a "careless, rimiss, flat, dry cold dead frame of spirit," while a colleague complained that "the Profession of so many hath run itself out of breath, and broke its neck in these dayes." Society was said to be paying a price for the faltering of faith: parents were letting their children "have their swinge, to go out and come when and where they please, especially in the night"; the young were flocking to "the Tavern and Ale-house and seldome away before Drunk or well-tipled."[5]

Many, however, denied that things were as bad as the preachers claimed. One original settler, for example, brought Increase Mather (1639–1723) up short in 1675 for dwelling on the drunkenness allegedly afflicting Massachusetts; conditions were worse at "the first beginning of the Colony," the oldtimer told Mather.[6] No one would argue that the spiritual intensity of the Puritans had, like their sobriety, increased over time, but this does not mean that religion in New England decayed as it matured. Having accommodated itself to changing conditions, religion was different towards the end of the seventeenth century than earlier, but it was healthy. According to one recent student, during the very years, 1675–90, when faith in New England was said to be in the doldrums, there occurred "a major revival in church membership—a turning to religion and the churches on a scale that had not been experienced since the first decade of settlement. The assumption that church membership steadily declined in the last three decades of the century is totally inaccurate."[7]

Recently, feminist historians have attacked the declension theory from another angle, arguing that it is sexist. Men, they point out, may have stopped joining churches but membership levels did not decline because large numbers of women continued to attain full communion in the Puritan and Quaker meetings. Religious declension in colonial America, a woman historian asserts, was a mirage, based "only on a loss of *male* piety."[8]

Even what look like objective accounts of the condition of religion in eighteenth-century America prove, on examination, to be misleading. In 1701, for example, George Keith informed Church of England authorities that, in New Jersey, there was "no face of any public Worship of any Sort," when, in fact, at the moment Keith wrote, there were forty-five congregations gathered and worshipping in private houses.[9] The key word here is "gathered," for a considerable amount of eighteenth-century religion was of the do-it-yourself variety, consisting of voluntary groups meeting by mutual agreement in barns or farmhouses under the care of a devout layman or schoolmaster who, on Sundays, read homilies or selections from collections of printed sermons. These groups, often close in spirit to primitive Christianity, existed in every colony, although they were far more numerous south of New England. Some German Reformed and Lutheran congregations in frontier Maryland, for example, operated for decades, until ordained ministers, who were greeted with "tears of joy," caught up with them.[10]

The Scotch-Irish Presbyterians were especially resolute in organizing frontier churches in the absence of ministers. Beginning in the second decade of the eighteenth century, these men and women came to the colonies from Northern Ireland in large numbers, perhaps as many as 250,000 by the Declaration of Independence. The stout faith of these immigrants has been proverbial—there is an old quip that, in the event of a crop failure, Scotch-Irish farmers could survive on the Westminster Shorter Catechism—but recent scholarship has put an even higher estimate on the strength of their religious convictions. Scotch-Irish Presbyterians now appear to have introduced as much religious energy into the eighteenth-century middle and southern colonies as the Puritans did in seventeenth-century New England. Indeed, one expert has asserted that "Scottish lay religiosity was probably more informed and systematic than even that in New England."[11] Scotch-Irish religious activity was less visible and more poorly recorded than that of the New England Puritans because much of it was shrouded in the wilderness of western Pennsylvania and points south, but when preachers reached a Scotch-Irish Presbyterian community, however remote, they found the people "well indoctrinated in the principles of the Christian religion" and almost always in the process of "forming themselves into something like ecclesiastical order."[12]

It is often touching to read accounts of the thirst for the Gospel of ordinary men and women in inaccessible parts of eighteenth-century America. Itinerant ministers who appeared on the frontier were begged to stay and subscriptions to pay their salaries were opened on the spot. Members of western congregations were "willing to sell their coats and the rest of their clothing to help support a preacher." Like modern real estate speculators, groups of believers built churches on speculation, hoping that a minister might be attracted by a brand new "brave Church of brick." At places that had churches, packed houses were reported, with listeners being "forced to stand without doors and others hanging out the window." Ministers reported families walking "10 to 12 Miles with their Children in the burning Sun, so earnest, so desirous [were they] of becoming good Christians." People deserted their homesteads to hear the Word: "several people have moved," one minister reported, "and gone elsewhere to the church seeing the church does not come to them." Others moved to different denominations, "being willing to embrace anything that looks like a religion, rather than have none at all." The people are "ready to devour Me," wrote an itinerant minister in the 1760s, summarizing the hunger for the Gospel in eighteenth-century America.[13]

The inability of the various denominations to keep up with an expanding population created what one recent scholar has called "a crisis of Christian

In Side of the Old Lutheran Church in 1800, York, Pa.
Watercolor with pen and ink by Lewis Miller (1796–1882).
Historical Society of York County, Pennsylvania.

This view of a Lutheran church by the Pennsylvania folk artist Lewis Miller spotlights homely features of worship in early America, such as the sexton chasing a dog out of the sanctuary and a member stoking up a stove.

practice."[14] This crisis (if it really was one) was fueled, to some extent, by fears along the Atlantic seaboard of the brutalizing effect of the frontier. There was an apprehension, that became much stronger in religious circles at the beginning of the nineteenth century, that moving into the wilderness might coarsen men to such an extent that they would eventually slip out of the Christian orbit altogether and become ungovernable by both church and state. Given the heroic efforts of many frontiersmen to keep the faith, these fears were exaggerated, but they were real nevertheless. Action was considered necessary to promote Christianity over the full extent of the country and the action had to come from such organizations as existed or could be created. Into this breach stepped state governments and the denominations themselves.

Early in the eighteenth century, several states marshaled their resources, modest as they often were, to empower the Anglican Church. The Church was established (supported by taxes) in New York City (1693), in Maryland (1702), in South Carolina (1706), and in North Carolina (1715). Simultaneously, the Society for the Propagation of the Gospel in Foreign Parts (SPG) was founded in England, which over the years sent six hundred Anglican priests to the American colonies, generously supplied with religious literature and paraphernalia. State support of religion was matched by the creation of denominational bureaucracies in the middle colonies, which also obtained pastors from Europe, established educational institutions that trained American ministers, raised money for the churches, and imposed standards that assured the integrity of ministers and the doctrine they preached. Philadelphia was the home of the denominational organizations: the Quaker Yearly Meeting (1686), the Presbytery of Philadelphia (1706), the Philadelphia

Baptist Association (1707), the Coetus of the German Reformed Church (1747), and the Lutheran Ministerium (1748).

The efforts of these organizations produced a sustained boom in church formation. Anglican churches increased from 111 in 1700 to 406 in 1780; the Baptists from 33 to 457; Congregationalists from 146 to 749; German and Dutch Reformed from 26 to 327; Lutherans from 7 to 240; and Presbyterians from 28 to 475.[15] And the colonists crowded these churches, estimates being that, between 1700 and 1740, between 74.7 and 80 percent of the population attended with some frequency.[16] These impressive figures belie any notion that religion was in retreat in the colonies in the eighteenth century, yet this theme continued to be irresistible to clergymen at all points of the religious spectrum, to none more than to the preachers who led the Great Awakening of 1734–45. The churches, these sons of thunder insisted, were suffering from "great Decay and Deadness."[17] Once again, however, it is important to discover what this indictment actually meant. A revivalist could lament that religion "lay as it were a dying" but could simultaneously assert that people were behaving in ways that would cause a modern minister to swell with pride, congregations being "pretty exact . . . in the Observance of the external Forms of Religion, not only as to Attendance upon publick Ordinances on the Sabbaths, but also, as the Practice of Family Worship, and perhaps secret Prayer too."[18] The point is that the revivalists echoed the preachers who were least in sympathy with them, the Anglican missionaries; the reports of both revealed that there was plenty of religion in the land, it was just not the kind that they liked.

A scholar has recently challenged the importance of the Great Awakening, pointing out that, for a century after it occurred, the nation's historians, including the formidable George Bancroft (1800–1891), ignored it, and suggesting that contemporary historians have made it greater than it was by using it as an "interpretative fiction" to weave together disparate elements in eighteenth-century history.[19] The Great Awakening was not a misnomer, however. It was great because it was an event—or rather a series of events—that had a wider scope and impact than any previous episode in American history. It was great because it was part of a movement that embraced the entire English-speaking world. And, finally, it was great because it created a style of religion—evangelicalism—whose "distinguishing marks," in the words of Jonathan Edwards, dominated the American spiritual landscape until the Civil War and continues to be a powerful factor in American religious life.

Evangelicalism is difficult to date and define. In 1531, at the beginning of the Reformation, Sir Thomas More (1478–1535) referred to religious adversaries as "Evaungelicalles," but scholars today consider evangelicalism as a self-conscious movement to have begun much later.[20] One expert claims that it began in the 1730s and that the leaders of the Great Awakening were among its pioneers.[21] Far from regarding themselves as innovators, however, the Awakeners saw themselves as theological throwbacks. Jonathan Edwards (1703–1758) asserted that he preached nothing but "the common plain Protestant doctrine of the Reformation."[22] The Methodists, following Wesley, said that they were "restoring the 'old divinity' of the Reformation."[23] Audiences who heard the Awakeners recognized that they were trying "to restore the Church to the Purity that she professt at the Dawn of the Reformation."[24]

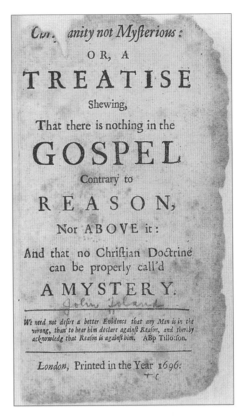

John Toland, *Christianity not Mysterious* (London, 1696). Rare Book and Special Collections Division.

John Toland (1670–1722) was one of a school of English and continental writers, loosely called deists, who commanded a following in eighteenth-century America, especially among statesmen like John Adams and Thomas Jefferson, who were receptive to Enlightenment ideas. Toland and like-minded writers held that religion was true only insofar as it was consistent with reason and that the mysterious and miraculous dimension of faith must be questioned. This position appealed to no more than a small minority of eighteenth-century Americans, whose sympathies lay overwhelmingly with the opposing evangelical view.

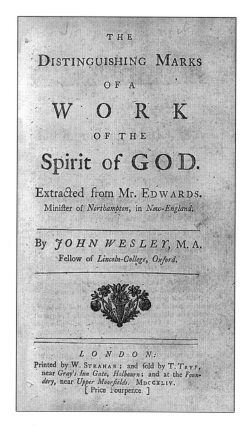

THE

DISTINGUISHING MARKS

OF A

WORK

OF THE

Spirit of GOD.

Extracted from Mr. EDWARDS.
Minister of *Northampton*, in *New-England*.

By *JOHN WESLEY*, M.A.
Fellow of *Lincoln-College, Oxford.*

LONDON:
Printed by W. STRAHAN; and sold by T. TRYE,
near *Gray's-Inn Gate, Holbourn*; and at the *Foun-
dery*, near *Upper Moorfields.* MDCXLIV.
[Price Fourpence.]

**John Wesley, *The Distinguishing Marks
of a Work of the Spirit of God.
Extracted from Mr. Edwards* (London, 1744).
Rare Book and Special Collections Division.**

*The publication by John Wesley of extracts from Jonathan
Edwards'* Distinguishing Marks *illustrates the trans-Atlantic
character of the Great Awakening. Revivals occurred between
1735–1745 in most parts of the English-speaking world:
England, Scotland, Wales, and the British North American
colonies. The leaders communicated with each other and, in
some cases, were personal acquaintances.*

Exactly what aspects of evangelicalism were grounded in the Reformation? First, there was a fresh, experimental interpretation of the ancient doctrine of original sin, promoted by John Calvin (1509–1564), which all eighteenth-century revivalists preached. Equally important was the concept of the conversion of the individual by divine power from sin to grace, the process Luther described as justification by faith. All writers on evangelicalism emphasize that conversion is its alpha and omega and they also emphasize that, in the evangelical view, a personally-felt conversion must be produced by the preaching of the Word, not by the administration of the sacraments. Evangelicalism had a special term for one who had been converted: he or she had received a "new birth." The concept of the "new birth," though as old as John's Gospel, was first widely used during the Reformation. It was much favored by the Puritans, who, as soon as they arrived in Massachusetts in the 1630s, required prospective church members to prove to an audience of the converted that they had experienced regeneration by undergoing the new birth. A succinct account of the objective of Great Awakening preachers, which reveals the strong links to the Reformation theology, was written by a Pennsylvania Presbyterian in 1744: "The Nature and Necessity of the New-Birth" involved "a Conviction of Sin and Misery, by the Holy Spirits opening and applying the Law to the Conscience, in order to a saving Closure with Christ."[25]

Many of the methods used by preachers during the Great Awakening had good Reformation pedigrees. One of them was bringing audiences to a "true sight" of their sins by describing in the most lurid terms the unspeakable consequences—eternal damnation—of their iniquity. During the Reformation, some preachers frowned on their brethren who kept their congregations "under terror," but many of the early Puritans did not shrink from using this technique. John Rogers (1572–1636), for example, who was much admired in New England as "one of the most Awakening preachers of the age," was described during the reign of James I as "taking hold with both hands at one time of the supporters of the Canopy over the Pulpit and roaring hideously, to represent the torments of the damned."[26] A line ran directly from Rogers through early New England preachers to Jonathan Edwards' grandfather, Solomon Stoddard (1643–1729), the eminent minister at Northampton, Massachusetts, who in 1713 published a sermon on the *Efficacy of the Fear of Hell*. Great theologian that he was, Edwards was a master of a singular kind of understated hellfire preaching, whose most famous example, preached during the Great Awakening at Enfield, Connecticut, was *Sinners in the Hands of an Angry God* (1742).

The preaching of terror by accomplished practitioners during the Great Awakening traumatized ordinary men and women, as the experience of a Connecticut farmer, Nathan Cole, attests. Returning from a revival in 1741 Cole wrote that "hell fire was almost always in my mind: and I have hundreds of times put my finger into my pipe when I have been smoking to feel how fire felt: and to see how my Body could bear to lye in Hell fire for ever and ever."[27]

Although Cole's anguish was acute, it is imperative to remember that the overwhelming majority of Awakeners were not sadistic bullies and that they intervened against colleagues who revelled in inflicting excessive psychological terror. Gilbert Tennent (1703–1764), for example, stopped a preacher scourging an audience with this comforting rejoinder: "is there no balm in Gilead? is there no physician?"[28]

For evangelical ministers, preaching hellfire was part of a carefully crafted strategy based on the Calvinists' respect for the strength of sin. Their audiences, they knew, might have a "Doctrinal Knowledge" of their spiritual thralldom, but unless they had a "feeling Sense" of their hopeless condition they were beyond help.[29] What the Awakeners dared to do was to enlist the emotions, the "affections," in the work of salvation, not merely the feelings of fear and despair, but—and this is often overlooked because less eye-catching—the raptures of joy and exaltation produced by the reception of grace.

There was precedent in early Puritan practice for the use of emotions, for, as Thomas Hooker (1586–1647) observed, a work of regeneration was a "holy kind of violence" that was bound to arouse the affections.[30] Some of the best Puritan preachers regularly aroused strong feelings. It was said, for example, of Thomas Shepard (1605–1649) "that he scarce ever preached a sermon, but some or other of his congregation were struck with great distress, and cried out in agony, what shall I do to be saved?"[31] On the other hand, Puritans of John Winthrop's stripe, recognizing that stimulating the emotions was playing with fire, strived to keep them on a short leash. Unlike Winthrop, the preachers of the Great Awakening were willing to gamble that giving the emotions full play would promote God's kingdom. They were prepared, therefore, to explain and justify as actions of the Spirit the harvests of mass emotions that they produced, the crowds of persons "crying out aloud, shrieking, being put into great Agonies of Body, and deprived of their bodily Strength, and the like," even as others danced, shouted and sang for joy.[32] Unlike other aspects of the Great Awakening, which were a repackaging of older doctrines and techniques, the emotions that

The Reverend Mr. George Whitefield A.M.
Mezzotint, 1769,
by John Greenwood (1727–1792),
after Nathaniel Hone.
National Portrait Gallery,
Smithsonian Institution.

This familiar image of the great evangelist reveals an eye problem that prompted unfriendly contemporaries to call him "Dr. Squintum." Some scholars doubt that Whitefield favored this "blessing posture."

George Whitefield's field pulpit.
American Tract Society, Garland, Texas.

Whitefield's oak field pulpit, collapsible and portable, was five and a half feet high and contained a rectangular platform two and a half feet square. Whitefield needed the pulpit for open-air preaching because the doors of many churches were closed against him. The first recorded use of the pulpit was at Moorsfield, England, April 9, 1742, where Whitefield preached to a crowd that he estimated at "twenty or thirty thousand people." Members of the audience who had come to the park for more frivolous pursuits showered the evangelist with "stones, rotten eggs and pieces of dead cat;" nothing daunted, he won many converts. It is estimated that Whitefield preached at least two thousand sermons from his field pulpit.

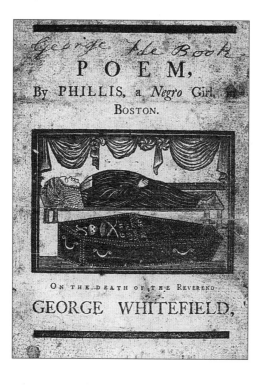

Burial of George Whitefield.
Woodcut for title page of *Poem By Phillis* [Wheatley], *a Negro Girl, in Boston. On the Death of the Reverend George Whitefield* (Boston, 1770).
Courtesy, American Antiquarian Society, Worcester, Massachusetts.

Whitefield's death and burial at Newburyport, Massachusetts, in 1770 made a deep impression on Americans from all walks of life. Among the eulogies composed for Whitefield was one from an unexpected source: a poem by a seventeen-year-old Boston slave, Phillis Wheatley (c. 1753–1784), who had only been in the colonies for nine years. Freed by her owners, Phillis Wheatley continued her literary career and was acclaimed as the "African poetess."

it generated, both in kind and degree, were new on the American religious landscape.

Just as new were the techniques brought to America by the evangelical prodigy, George Whitefield (1714–1770), whose tour of the country in 1739 electrified the populations of several colonies. Whitefield has emerged in recent scholarship as a figure every bit as important as his admirers believed him to be. Modern writers, it is true, have not hailed him, as some in the eighteenth century did, as a "God come down in the likeness of Man,"[33] but they have called him America's first cultural hero and compared his influence to George Washington's.[34] How did this young, British-born Anglican priest—Whitefield was twenty-five when he began achieving his great triumphs in America— make such a gigantic impact?

In the first place, Whitefield was an old-fashioned Calvinist, who, according to Benjamin Franklin (1706–1790), addressed his audiences as "half beasts and half devils," music to the theological ears of the Presbyterians of the middle colonies and the Congregationalists of New England. Next, Whitefield had the mystique of a rebel, for he regularly thumbed his nose at the hierarchy of his own Church of England, always resented and feared by the non-Anglican population in America. Nothing played better in many parts of the colonies than Whitefield's charge that Archbishop Tillotson knew "no more of true religion than Mahomet."[35] Finally, and most importantly, Whitefield's popularity rested on innovations he introduced into the revivalists' repertoire.

Whitefield grasped the importance of advertising that was revolutionizing the world of commerce in his native Britain, and employed this powerful new tool to revolutionize the presentation of the Word. He promoted his forthcoming appearances by planting stories in local newspapers, often written by himself, which stressed his previous triumphs, and he used what today would be called public relations techniques to flood preaching venues with his published sermons and religious travelogues. Thus, Whitefield's audiences were primed for a transforming religious experience, which usually occurred in a self-fulfilling way.

Another new Whitefield tactic was what critics derided as "Mobb preaching," the preference for speaking on village greens, in public squares, anywhere the Gospel could be brought to the greatest number of people.[36] Once assembled, Whitefield's listeners experienced the Word in a new way; rather than read his sermons or speak from notes, as was customary at the time, Whitefield preached extemporaneously, using simple, non-technical words, pitched to the understanding of the humblest listener, a language one recent scholar has called "egalitarian."[37] Finally, as a lover of the theater, Whitefield brought the methods of the stage to the pulpit so successfully that John Adams (1735–1826), who first heard him as a teenager, saluted him as "that great model of theatrical grace."[38] Whitefield made preaching a performance in which the great drama of salvation was acted out with the use of bodily gestures and vocal modulations designed to stimulate the emotions of the viewer and produce the new birth.

Whitefield's arsenal of advertising, theatrical showmanship, message simplification, emotional stimulation, and non-denominationalism has impressed scholars as being so modern that it "would . . . characterize evangelicalism into the twentieth century."[39] A recent writer has, in fact, likened Whitefield to today's televangelists.[40] To make Whitefield comprehensible to a modern audience, a scholar has compared his revivals to "the civil rights demonstrations, the campus disturbances, and the urban riots of the 1960s combined."[41] Another comparison is also possible: a captivating young Britisher from a modest background, rebelling against authority, performing in a new style with a new voice, using clever self-promotion to draw huge, emotionally charged crowds in one American city after another—Whitefield and his entourage might, without doing too much violence to the facts, be called the Beatles with Bibles.

Whitefield's tour of the colonies from December 1739 to January 1741 was the zenith of the Great Awakening. In New England in the fall of 1740, he drew unprecedented crowds—thirty thousand were said to have heard his farewell sermon in Boston—great numbers of whom, according to a local minister, "were so happily concerned about their souls, as we have never seen anything like it before."[42] At times, the revival brought all business to a halt. Upon his departure, Whitefield deputized his friend, the Presbyterian Gilbert Tennent, to come from New Jersey to New England to "blow up the divine fire lately kindled there."[43] Tennent had Whitefield's passion and conviction, but none of his polish and stage presence, and was, accordingly, lampooned as "an awkward and ridiculous Ape of Whitefield . . . roaring and bellowing, Hell, Damnation, Devils."[44] The revivals, nevertheless, continued to prosper in both New England and the middle colonies, until they began losing momentum in 1742. Tennent was part of the problem because he indulged an abusive streak in his personality (later corrected) by reviling opponents with choice epithets like "dead Dogs," a practice that alienated many friends of the Awakening. In a famous sermon, *The Danger of an Unconverted Ministry* (1740), Tennent lashed out at "Pharisee-Shepherds" who "with the Craft of Foxes . . . did not forget to breathe forth the Cruelty of Wolves, in a malicious Aspersing the Person of Christ."[45] What should Christians suffering under an uncon-

verted ministry do? Tennent advised them that it was lawful to leave the church and to seek living waters elsewhere. Many New Englanders did precisely this, producing divisions in at least 125 Congregational churches. The seceders and friends of the revival who remained in the churches were called New Lights. Their opponents were the Old Lights.

Some Old Lights had become beguiled by efforts of European thinkers to reconcile religion with the Enlightenment. In 1743 New England's leading spokesman for this group, Charles Chauncey (1705–1787), asserted in an anti-Awakening polemic that "the Plain Truth is [that] an enlightened Mind, not raised Affections, ought always to be the Guide" of Christians.[46] An enlightened mind, which soon became the ideal of New England Old Lights and Anglican ministers in many parts of America, led to a religious outlook that has been variously and indiscriminately called "Enlightenment religious liberalism," rational religion, or deism. Deism is of interest in America not because of the numbers who professed it, at best a "minority within a minority,"[47] nor because, in the nineteenth century, its adherents were among those who coalesced into a modest new denomination—Unitarianism—grounded, according to the old joke, in the Fatherhood of God, the Brotherhood of Man, and the Neighborhood of Boston. Rather its interest lies in the stature of the people who are alleged by various scholars to have embraced it—Washington, Jefferson, Adams, Franklin, and Hamilton, as well as other Founding Fathers.

The enlightened mind, touted by Chauncey and later devotees, was hospitable to reason and science, which the eighteenth-century philosophers presented as panaceas for the human condition. Religion, no less than phenomena in the physical universe, must undergo rigorous analysis and be vali-

Baptism in the Schuylkill River. Woodcut from Morgan Edwards,
Materials Towards a History of the American Baptists **(Philadelphia, 1770).**
The Historical Society of Pennsylvania, Philadelphia.

Baptists differed from other major American protestant denominations by offering baptism (by immersion) only to those who had under-gone a conversion experience; infants were, therefore, excluded from the sacrament, an issue that generated acrimonious controversy with fellow Christians. Baptists enjoyed remarkable growth from the Great Awakening onward, becoming, with the Methodists, the largest denomination in the nation by the mid-nineteenth century.

dated by reason. Such scrutiny often led deists to stray from the fundamentals of the faith. They viewed Christ along a spectrum, at the low end considering him as a human being teaching a "sub-lime" system of morality, at the higher end taking the Arian position that, though less than God, Christ was a pre-existing Divine Savior. They generally believed that God created the world, required men to act according to the Golden Rule, and imposed judgment in an afterlife.

Benjamin Franklin, the embodiment of the En-lightenment in America, spoke as a deist when, in the last days of his life, he confided to Ezra Stiles that he had "with most Dissenters in England, some

Doubts as to [Christ's] Divinity."[48] The unusual thing about Franklin's statement was that he made it at all. So strong was the power of religious ortho-doxy to compel conformity in eighteenth-century America that the Founding Fathers obsessively con-cealed their religious opinions, if tinctured ever so slightly by the unconventional. The result has been a cottage industry among historians trying to puzzle out the religious convictions of the Founders, lead-ing to a stream of publications on such topics as "Was Alexander Hamilton a Christian Statesman?"[49]

Hamilton (1755–1804), in fact, is an instruc-tive example of the perils of pinning religious labels on the Founders. In college and as a young officer

*The Revd. Francis Asbury. Bishop of the
Methodist Episcopal Church in the United States.*
**Engraving by Benjamin Tanner, after John W. Paradise,
Philadelphia, March, 1814.
Prints and Photographs Division (LC-USZC4-6153).**

Francis Asbury (1745–1816), who came to America from his native England as a Methodist missionary in 1771, become the dynamo who drove the spectacular growth of the Methodist church after the Revolutionary War. During his ministry he ordained 4,000 ministers, preached 16,000 sermons, and traveled 270,000 miles on horseback, sometimes to the most inaccessible parts of the United States.

in the Continental Army he was in the "habit of praying on his knees night and day" and impressed friends as a "zealous believer in the fundamental doctrines of Christianity."[50] There is little information about Hamilton's religious views during mid-life. On his death bed we find him imploring an Episcopal bishop to administer Holy Communion. When and in what sense can he be considered a deist?

The same question can be asked about George Washington (1732–1799), who is often described as a deist. Washington left behind no written evidence about his private religious convictions. Judging from his public conduct, he was a loyal Episcopalian. If he was a deist, he did not consider his views incompatible with full participation in his church, because for years he served faithfully as a member of his local vestry. The larger point here is that deism in America, such as it was, did not veer off into anti-clericalism, as it did in Europe; it accommodated itself, without exception, to existing religious institutions.

Deism certainly did not drain members off from the local churches, which continued to be remarkably robust on the eve of the American Revolution, contrary to the persistent notion that religion in eighteenth-century America was progressively declining. A century ago, a writer claimed that, during and after the Revolution, Christianity was "at the lowest low-water mark of the lowest ebb tide."[51] Other writers have simply said that religion during the Revolutionary Era was in a state of "depression." A recent study of church attendance reveals, however, that in 1776 between 71 and 77 percent of Americans may have filled the pews on Sunday.[52] Another scholar's research indicates that, "far from suffering decline, religion experienced vigorous growth and luxuriant development during the Revolutionary period." "It is more accurate," continues this writer, "to characterize the years between 1775 and 1790 as a Revolutionary revival," the return, on a smaller scale, of the Great Awakening.[53]

Although the Awakening petered out in New England and in the middle colonies in the mid-1740s, the supporters of the revivals in those areas, the New Lights in New England and their theological soulmates, the New Side Presbyterians in the middle colonies, consolidated their strength in similar ways. Some New England New Lights, who initially separated from the established Congregational churches, returned to the fold. Many more, however, became Separate Baptists who absorbed the region's previously unfriendly "Old Baptist" churches and refreshed them with the evangelical spirit. The new denomination boomed, attracting by 1786 forty thousand converts from other New England churches. Among these were many women, who, bonded during the Great Awakening with their fellow Baptists in the spiritual egalitarianism of the new birth, acquired unprecedented authority in church governance. These gains, it has been argued recently, were rolled back by the impact of the American Revolution, which, though fought in the name of liberating the American people from oppression, had the ironic result, in the religious sphere, of subjecting women to "gender subordination."[54]

The New Side Presbyterians also absorbed their Old Side adversaries. After the denomination split in 1741 the Old Side stagnated, while the New Side flourished, because of its ability to train its own ministers in crude but intellectually demanding "Log Colleges"—one of which evolved into Princeton University—and because of the evangelical sympathies of the Scotch-Irish immigrants who continued to swarm into the middle colonies. Recent investigations of the Scotch-Irish have revealed them as the prototypical Anglo-American revivalists. Large-scale, passionate revivals, discovered in Ulster as early as 1625, occurred with regularity thereafter in both Ulster and in Scotland itself, usually at three- to four-day "communion seasons."[55] George Whitefield preached at a revival in Scotland in 1742 that "far outdid all that I ever saw in America. For about an hour and a half there was such weeping and so many falling into deep distress . . . that description is impossible. The people seemed to be smitten by scores. They were carried off and brought into the house like wounded soldiers taken from a field of battle."[56] People bred on this sort of religious experience would naturally gravitate to the New Side in America. And, as they and their kinsmen spread along the frontiers of Pennsylvania, Virginia, and North Carolina, and then over the mountains into Kentucky, they left a powder trail ready to be ignited by the first evangelical preachers who could catch up with them. The New and Old Side Presbyterians merged in 1758 but it was really a takeover by the New Siders. They had far more ministers, 73 to 22, than the Old Side and set the tone for the reunited denomination.

Emerging from the Awakening, the Presbyterians and Baptists were self-confident and energetic, in full fighting trim, ready to sally forth and battle Satan in his southern strongholds. Beginning in the 1740s, New Side Presbyterian revivalists, led by Samuel Davies (1723–1761), began "shaking the dry bones" in central Virginia. They were followed in the next decade by New England Separate Baptists, led by Shubal Stearns (1706–1771), who kindled a fervent revival at Sandy Creek, North Carolina. Throughout the remainder of the century, Presbyterians and Baptists poured missionaries into the south—in 1789 the Baptist patriarch himself,

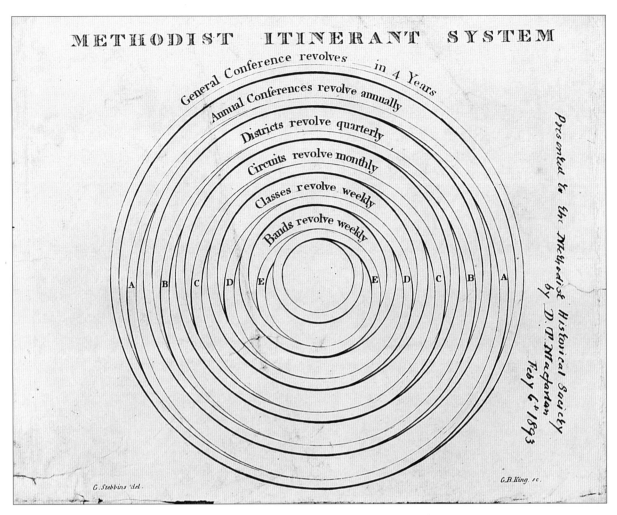

G. Stebbins and G. B. King, *Methodist Itinerant System*. Broadside, New York, 1810–11(?). Rare Books Division, New York Public Library, Astor, Lenox and Tilden Foundation.

The remarkable growth of the Methodists in the post-Revolutionary period was attributed by many to a hierarchical organizational structure that seemed to be peculiarly suited to American conditions. The "corporating genius" of the Methodists is depicted in this series of concentric circles.

Isaac Backus (1724–1806), conducted a five-month mission in North Carolina and Virginia—setting in motion a cycle of revivals that rolled well into the nineteenth century.

Baptists and Presbyterians found easy pickings in the Anglican south, where a rationalistic clergy preached "little else but morality. The great doctrines of universal depravity, redemption by the blood of Christ [and] regeneration" seemed, according to the invading evangelists, to be relics of an earlier age.[57] The revivalists imitated Whitefield's stage mannerisms—one celebrated Baptist minister, John Leland (1754–1841), was accused of being too "theatrical"—and they preached his brand of old-fashioned Calvinism, stressing the sin from which mankind must be "awakened" before conversion was possible.[58] An Anglican priest, soured by seeing his parishioners picked off by the revivalists, assailed Presbyterian evangelists for preaching the "terrors of the law, cursing & scolding, calling the old people Grey headed Devils, and all promiscuously, Damn'd double damn'd . . . Lumps of hellfire, incarnate Devils, 1000 times worse than devils, etc."[59] Displays of mass emotion followed these fusillades, as they had in New England and the middle colonies, but the "celestial discord among the people" did not ruffle the evangelists, who considered it a prelude to the reception of the Holy Spirit and the advent of the new birth.

Only on the eve of the American Revolution did the Methodists, founded in England by John Wesley (1703–1791) in the 1730s as a reform movement within the Church of England, begin to make their mark. Their first circuit was not established in Virginia until 1774, but the next year they led a revival in the central part of the state that, by 1778, produced three new circuits there and in North Carolina. Nothing could stop the Methodists, not even being stigmatized as Tories because of Wesley's opposition to the American Revolution. By 1780 they had 106 churches, by 1790, 712. During this same period Separate Baptists brought the "Revolutionary revival" to northern New England by leading the "New Light stir" which spread from the Merrimac Valley in Massachusetts in 1779 to Maine, New Hampshire, and western Massachusetts by 1784. Meanwhile, Presbyterians reaped a "rich harvest of converts" in the Cumberland Valley of Pennsylvania and in southern Virginia.[60]

The accelerating activity of Presbyterians, Baptists, and Methodists during and after the American Revolution changed the country's religious landscape, for by the early decades of the nineteenth century these were the three largest denominations in the United States. How different the scene in 1740 when Anglicans, Quakers, and Congregationalists were the big three of American religion. These groups were eclipsed because they were either outright opponents of the Great Awakening (the Anglicans and the Quakers) or because they were divided by it (the Congregationalists). Evangelicalism emerged from the Awakening as the force of the future in American religion; those groups on the wrong side of it were driven to the sidelines. If evangelicalism experienced a "burgeoning prosperity"[61] on the eve of the American Revolution, the nation had seen nothing yet, for, during the first half of the nineteenth century, it became such a dominant force that historians have used terms such as "golden day"[62] to describe its sovereignty in American religious life. Indeed, so large does evangelicalism loom that some scholars complain that their colleagues have overemphasized its power as an "explanatory device," attributing to its influence everything from Jacksonian Democracy to the Civil War.[63]

What of George Whitefield, the architect of the evangelical triumph? After leaving America at the height of the Awakening in 1741, Whitefield made four more trips to the country, the longest lasting from 1744 to 1748. Although he never again orchestrated a revival comparable to the Awakening, his enormous popularity in America never waned. A remarkable incident at the beginning of the Revolutionary War testifies to the great evangelist's hold on the imagination of ordinary Americans. In the fall of 1775, a New England force, commanded by Benedict Arnold (1741–1801), was recruited to invade Canada and capture Quebec. Arriving in Newburyport, Massachusetts, where Whitefield had been buried in 1770, the officers descended into the church crypt, opened Whitefield's coffin, removed his clerical collar and wristbands, cut them in pieces, and passed them out to the troops. The distribution of these Great Awakening amulets showed in its eerie way that men facing stress and anxiety wanted links to a preacher of a living God, not the latest London edition of Locke.[64] One need look no farther for the reason evangelicalism demolished deism in eighteenth-century America.

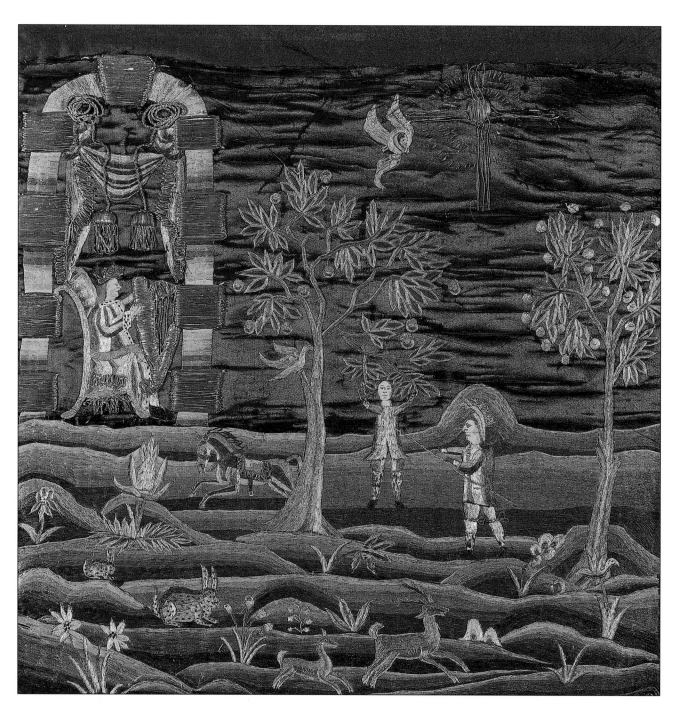

The Hanging of Absalom. Needlework (silk and metal thread on black satin, with painted details) by Faith Robinson Trumbull, c. 1770. Lyman Allyn Art Museum, New London, Connecticut.

Apparently created soon after the Boston Massacre, this needlework is an excellent example of the way in which many colonists understood political events in terms of familiar biblical stories. Apparently, the creator of the work, Faith Robinson Trumbull (1718–1780), understood Absalom to be a patriot, rebelling against and suffering from the arbitrary rule of his father King David (George III), shown at the top left, playing his harp, evidently oblivious to the anguish of his children in the American colonies. Joab, slaying Absalom with a spear, is dressed as a British redcoat, specifically as one of the British soldiers who fired into the crowd in Boston on March 5, 1770. Recently, a scholar has suggested that this work was created somewhat earlier by Mrs. Trumbull's daughter.

THREE ❧

RELIGION AND THE AMERICAN REVOLUTION

The continuation of the revivals spawned by the Great Awakening into the era of the American Revolution has raised the question of whether these two seminal events were related. A few scholars have even suggested that the Revival may have "caused" the Revolution. Although experts have scoffed at this theory, it has had a staying power not unlike the notion that religion was decaying in eighteenth-century America; in modified forms, it continues to find occasional adherents.

It was the victims of the Revolution, the Tories, who paid the political power of religion its highest compliment—in their view its highest reproach—by identifying it as the principal cause of the rebellion against George III (1738–1820). Initially, the Tories denounced local clergymen for allowing themselves to become the dupes of incendiaries like Samuel Adams (1722–1803) and for inflaming their congregations against the King and his ministers. As the dispute with the mother country became more intractable, however, the Tories persuaded themselves that the difficulties ran deeper than the rant-

ings of "some mad Preachers." They concluded that the problem was structural, that certain of the colonies' religious denominations were, by doctrine and tradition, inherently subversive and could never peaceably coexist with monarchical government, against which they had now risen in arms, as their ancestors had done in England in the 1640s.

The former speaker of the Pennsylvania Assembly, Joseph Galloway (1731–1803), expressed this view in 1780, when he blamed the conflagration on "republican sectaries" by whom he meant Presbyterians and Congregationalists "whose principles of religion and polity [were] equally averse to those of the established Church and Government."[1] In the same year, the Anglican clergy of New York claimed it as a "certain Truth . . . that Dissenters in general, and particularly Presbyterians and Congregationalists were active Promoters of the Rebellion," the explanation being that "from their Infancy [they] imbibe Republican, levelling Principles, which are unfriendly to the Constitution, and lead them to an opposite Conduct."[2]

Although Presbyterians and Congregationalists

have doted on the accusation that they were the original American democrats, professional historians have been unwilling to concede them a monopoly on revolutionary patriotism. The old Tory idea that certain kinds of religion were politically subversive has been revived, however, by scholars trying to establish a relationship between the Great Awakening and the American Revolution. They argue that evangelicalism itself, divorced from any denominational setting, had a "revolutionary potential" that fueled the conflict with Great Britain.[3]

A principal proponent of this view sees the connection between evangelicalism and politics luminously appearing in the "uprising of the 1770s," which impressed him as "not so much the result of reasoned thought as an emotional outburst similar to a religious revival."[4] Others assert that those experiencing the new birth in the 1740s were at the same time converted to anti-authoritarianism, which they honed in battles with the established churches and the political authorities aligned with them. The impulse to defy authority, it is argued, was transferred to British officials when their policies became oppressive in the 1760s, and contributed to the rebellion a decade later.

The notion that evangelicalism was inherently anti-authoritarian has not survived close scrutiny. In the 1740s the Presbyterian New Side revivalists separated from the Old Side because they wanted their denomination to exercise more, not less, discipline over the faithful. "Pro-authoritarian," the revivalists formed their own synod to exercise "coercive power" that the opponents of the revival could not stomach.[5] The Methodists took an even higher view of denominational authority, their remarkable growth in post-Revolutionary America being fostered by a tight disciplinary apparatus that resembled "a military mission of short term agents."

Their leader, Francis Asbury, was denounced by a former sympathizer, as having a "strong passion for superiority and thirst for domination."[6]

The flaws in the theory that evangelical religion was the motor of the Revolution become even more apparent if the political role of its theological adversaries, the Liberals, is examined. The evangelicals-as-revolutionaries theory pictures the Liberals as political conservatives who were lukewarm supporters of the Revolution. But the evidence reveals that the Liberals furnished many of the most radical revolutionaries: Thomas Paine (1737–1809), Thomas Jefferson, Dr. Thomas Young, Samuel Adams, Ebenezer McIntosh, and Ethan Allen (1738–1789). It would be wrong to say that the Liberals were the leaders, the evangelicals the followers, in instigating the American Revolution, but the reverse of the statement would be equally untrue; the case for evangelicalism as the engine of the American Revolution simply cannot be made.

To de-emphasize the revolutionary role of evangelicalism does not, in any way, mean that religion played no role in the American Revolution. Recent scholarship has reinforced the traditional view of its relationship to the Revolution, namely, that although religion did not directly cause the revolt against Britain—which is now seen as a conflict over political-constitutional ideas—it offered powerful support to the American cause at every step of the way.

Aside from Anglicans in the north, preachers of every denomination supported the Revolution; they were "almost universally good Whigs," said New Jersey Governor William Livingston (1723–1790) in 1790.[7] That ministers should have played a role in the Revolution is not surprising, for it was customary, in most colonies, for clergymen to interest themselves in politics. Although tradition forbade them, in most places, to hold public office, in New England and elsewhere ministers regularly delivered sermons to newly elected legislators in which they commented, openly or obliquely, on the issues of the day. Militia musters, fasts, and thanksgiving days also gave ministers the opportunity to discuss public events.

Some ministers were outspoken advocates of "preaching politics." One such was Jonathan Mayhew (1720–1766), pastor of the West Church, Boston, who combined extreme liberalism in theology with radicalism in politics. Unable to abide the status quo in either church or state, Mayhew was the prototype of later generations of American ministers who have used their clerical status as a passport to plunge into politics. Death defined the man, for his demise was attributed by his admirers to his being "overplied by public energies."[8]

In 1750, reflecting on the execution of Charles I (1600–1649), Mayhew delivered one of the most famous American sermons of the eighteenth century, *A Discourse Concerning Unlimited Submission*, in which he impatiently explored the idea that Christians were obliged to suffer under an oppressive ruler, as some Anglicans argued. Nonsense, said Mayhew; resistance to a tyrant was a "glorious" Christian duty. In offering moral sanction for political resistance, Mayhew anticipated the position his brethren in all denominations took throughout the conflict with Britain. The idea was expressed in various ways, a typically impassioned example being a sermon preached by a Presbyterian minister, Abraham Keteltas, in 1777, in which the American effort was celebrated as "the cause of truth, against error and falsehood . . . the cause of pure and undefiled religion, against bigotry, superstition, and human inventions . . . in short, it is the cause of heaven against hell—of the kind Parent of the universe against the prince of darkness, and the destroyer of the human race."[9]

Jonathan Mayhew, D.D. Pastor of the West Church in Boston. **Etching by Giovanni Cipriani, London, 1767. American Antiquarian Society, Worcester, Massachusetts.**

An eloquent proponent of the idea that civil and religious liberty was the cause of God, Mayhew considered the Church of England as a dangerous, almost a diabolical, enemy of the New England way. The bishop's mitre with the snake emerging from it represented his view of the Anglican hierarchy.

Antisejanus. Drink deep, or taste not the Porterial Spring. Etching [1765].
Prints and Photographs Division (LC-USZ62-45398).

This satire is directed at the political parsons in both Britain and America who injected themselves into the controversy between the King and the colonies, in this case into the dispute over the Stamp Act. The satirist believes that clergymen, like monkeys in toyshops, cause mischief because of their ignorance of the political world. To them he dedicates Pope's couplet: "a little learning is a dangerous thing; drink deep, or taste not the Pierian spring." Learning is seen going to waste as it pours out of a keg labeled Trinity College; the parson does not deign to use his tankard to sample it.

The plain fact is that, had American clergymen of all denominations not assured their pious countrymen, from the beginning of the conflict with Britain, that the resistance movement was right in God's sight and had His blessing, it could not have been sustained and independence could not have been achieved. Here is the fundamental, the indispensable, contribution of religion and its spokesmen to the coming of the American Revolution.

Mayhew's assertion that resistance to political oppression was acceptable to God was an old idea that could be found in Elizabethan polemics. What made Mayhew such a formidable political pamphleteer was his mastery of contemporary British and continental writing. Many of his clerical brethren were equally at home in this literature, for the ministry was the closest thing the colonies had to an intellectual class, capable of consuming, processing, and disseminating avant-garde information. By the 1740s American clergymen were lacing their sermons with Locke's writings on the social compact and natural rights and were using the theories of British "opposition" writers like John Trenchard (1662–1723) and Thomas Gordon (d. 1750), who warned against the insatiable aggressiveness of political power. Consequently, when George III's ministry introduced its political reforms, including taxation of the colonies, in the 1760s, the clergy, conversant with the newest and best British and continental political science, saw how high the stakes were and how acute the danger was for America and were able to explain the crisis convincingly to their congregations. Other groups of Americans—lawyers, for example—also sounded the alarm, but, by combining Whig political theory with religious doctrine, the preachers forged an especially powerful weapon to mobilize opposition to British policies. Recently, a scholar has astutely observed that "by turning colonial resistance into a righteous

An Attempt to land a Bishop in America.
Engraving from the *Political Register*
(London, September 1769).
Prints and Photographs Division
(LC-USZ61-78).

The plot, as many colonists supposed, to impose Anglican bishops on America is thwarted in this cartoon by an indignant New England mob pushing a bishop's boat back towards England, frightening its prelate into praying, "Lord, now lettest thou thy Servant depart in Peace." The mob flings a volume of Calvin's Works at the bishop, while brandishing copies of Locke and Sydney on Government. It also shouts slogans: "Liberty & Freedom of Conscience"; "No Lords Spiritual or Temporal in New England"; and "Shall they be obliged to maintain Bishops that cannot maintain themselves."

cause, and by crying the message to all ranks in all parts of the colonies, ministers did the work of secular radicalism and did it better."[10]

It was not, in the final analysis, the clergy's skill in explicating Locke and Montesquieu that influenced their congregations so much as it was their ability to relate current events to the Bible, the frame of reference in which ordinary Americans understood the world. A recent study has illustrated this point in a striking fashion; an investigator has discovered a needlepoint work, completed by a

Connecticut housewife after the Boston Massacre of 1770, which depicts the colonies as Absalom being killed by a figure dressed as a British redcoat, for rebelling against the unpopular policies of his father, King David.[11] Revolutionary pamphleteers recognized that the best way to produce conviction was to pack their productions with biblical language. A freethinker like Thomas Paine (1737–1809) understood this point as well as the most pious hack. A principal reason for the unparalleled impact of *Common Sense* (1776) was Paine's extensive use of the

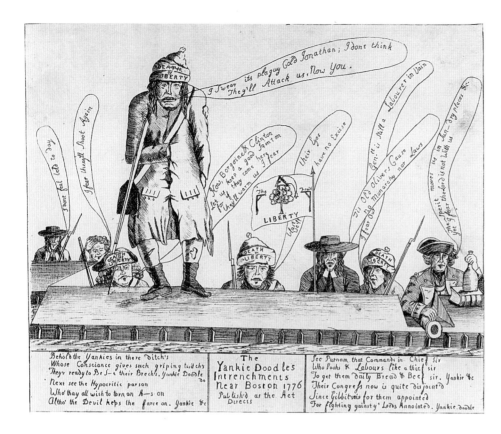

Bible to prove that the British monarchy was illegitimate, that it could not be "defended on the authority of Scripture; for the will of the Almighty, as declared by Gideon and the prophet Samuel expressly disapproves of government by kings."[12] Paine's readers informed him that, like the Apostle Paul on the road to Damascus, they were "blind but on reading these enlightening words the scales have fallen from our eyes" and they could see the way to independence.[13]

Clergymen were, of course, the real virtuosi in putting political events into a biblical context. By continually comparing George III and his ministers to such familiar—and hateful—biblical figures as Rehoboam and Pharaoh's taskmasters, they personalized and intensified the quarrel with Britain for their listeners. As the final rupture with the mother country approached, preachers of all denominations painted the lurid picture of Britain as the Beast in Revelations 13 who would annihilate the children of God. The conflict was now presented from the pulpits as a cosmic battle between good and evil in which no Christian could be neutral. The man in the pew must put on his gospel armor and take the field against the foe.[14]

Preachers seemed to vie with their brethren in other colonies in arousing their congregations against George III. In 1775, John Adams informed friends in New England that the ministers of Philadelphia "thunder and lighten every Sabbath" against British tyranny, while Jefferson reported that in Virginia "pulpit oratory ran 'like a shock of electricity' through the whole colony."[15] In this atmosphere, it is not surprising that a British agent in New York in March 1776 concluded that "at Bottom [this] was very much a religious War,"[16] an observation supported recently by a British historian who has called the American Revolution "the last great war of religion in the western world."[17]

Also propelling the American clergy into the

**Abraham Keteltas, *God Arising and Pleading His People's Cause*
(Newburyport, Massachusetts, 1777).
American Imprints,
Rare Book and Special Collections Division.**

Aside from the clergymen of the Church of England, most American ministers believed that the war against Great Britain was "the Cause of God" and, as such, made the armed participation of their congregations morally justifiable.

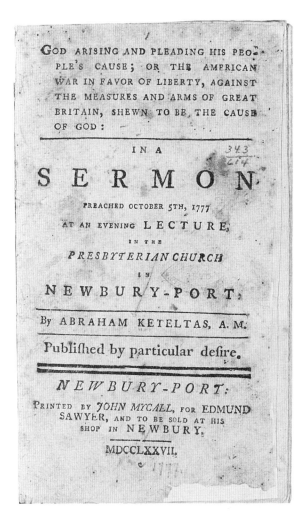

GOD ARISING AND PLEADING HIS PEO-
PLE'S CAUSE; OR THE AMERICAN
WAR IN FAVOR OF LIBERTY, AGAINST
THE MEASURES AND ARMS OF GREAT
BRITAIN, SHEWN TO BE THE CAUSE
OF GOD:

IN A

SERMON

PREACHED OCTOBER 5TH, 1777,

AT AN EVENING LECTURE,

IN THE

PRESBYTERIAN CHURCH

IN

NEWBURY-PORT;

By ABRAHAM KETELTAS, A.M.

Published by particular desire.

NEWBURY-PORT:

PRINTED BY *JOHN MYCALL*, FOR EDMUND
SAWYER, AND TO BE SOLD AT HIS
SHOP IN NEWBURY.

MDCCLXXVII.

**Gostelowe Standard No. 10, Armed Resistance.
Photograph of a watercolor once in
possession of Edward W. Richardson.
Courtesy of Pennsylvania Society of Sons of the
Revolution and Its Color Guard,
Philadelphia, Pennsylvania.**

*Many battle flags of the American Revolution, like the one shown
in this modern recreation, carried religious inscriptions.*

John Peter Gabriel Muhlenberg.
Oil on canvas by an unidentified American artist,
nineteenth century.
Collection of the Martin Art Gallery,
Muhlenberg College, Allentown, Pennsylvania.

Muhlenberg (1746–1807) and James Caldwell (1734–1781)
were among the numerous colonial ministers who took to the field
against the British. Muhlenberg had the most successful military
career of any "fighting parson."

conflict with Britain was a perceived threat to its institutional status, a threat posed by fears that piggy-backing on British political reforms was a plan to impose Anglican bishops on America. Although the British political establishment never supported this scheme, alarms about the appointment of American bishops—who were needed to ordain colonial priests—had been sounded as early as 1702. Anxieties increased in the 1760s when American Anglicans built a fancy house in Cambridge, Massachusetts, that was thought to be a "bishop's palace" and floated trial balloons in New York City that the colonists should be taxed to support the bishops in proper style. The prospect of bishops in America aroused atavistic fears of religious persecution of the kind that had driven the ancestors of many colonists from Europe, for it was widely assumed, despite Anglican denials, that bishops would bring with them the same ecclesiastical courts that had tortured and murdered dissenters in earlier times.

Ministers and laymen in various parts of the colonies filled the newspapers with what today seem to be hysterical denunciations of the purported plot to put them in bondage to bishops. To protect itself, the clergy recognized that it must man the political ramparts, for, if the King's ministers succeeded in establishing unlimited political power in America, all colonial institutions, including the churches, would be at their mercy. The bishop scheme was, in fact, seen as an "ecclesiastical stamp act"; if Britain achieved its goals of "taking away the liberty of taxing ourselves, and breaking in upon our charters," what, asked a Massachusetts New Light minister, would prevent her from compelling us "to support the pride and vanity of diocesan Bishops"?[18] Therefore, colonial ministers, including some southern Anglicans, waded into the political arena to secure their self-interest; they were determined that Anglican bishops would not

Reverend James Caldwell at the Battle of Springfield. Oil painting by Henry Alexander Ogden, undated. Presbyterian Historical Society, Philadelphia, Pennsylvania.

Caldwell is shown distributing Watts' Hymn Books to be used for wadding for the rifles of American soldiers at the battle of Springfield, June 23, 1780. Caldwell's wife was killed during Knyphausen's invasion of New Jersey in June 1780 and he himself was killed the next year at Elizabethtown Point, New Jersey.

make them dissenters in their own land, lord it over them, and persecute them, as Archbishop Laud and his minions had done in the bad, old—and not too distant—days of the Stuart kings.

During the War of Independence, some colonial ministers took the field against the British. A number enlisted as privates, like the Reverend John Cleaveland (1722–1799) of Ipswich, Massachusetts, who was sworn in on the same day as his four sons. Others commanded military units. The Reverend Phillips Payson (1736–1801) of Chelsea, Massachusetts, led a group of parishioners into battle at Lexington in 1775. Presbyterian ministers David Caldwell (1725–1824) and John Hull commanded units in North Carolina, Hull mounting a cavalry expedition against Cornwallis. The most conspicuous example of a fighting parson was Peter Muhlenberg, eldest son of the Lutheran patriarch, Henry Melchior Muhlenberg (1711–1787), who, in January 1776, at the conclusion of a sermon to his congregation in Woodstock, Virginia, threw off his clerical robes and displayed the uniform of an officer in the Virginia militia. Having served with distinction throughout the war, Muhlenberg commanded a brigade that successfully stormed the British lines at Yorktown. He retired from the army in 1783 as a brevetted major general.

Ministers eagerly sought chaplaincies in the Continental Army and the state militias. Some of them, such as the Presbyterian pastor James Caldwell of Elizabeth, New Jersey, could scarcely be restrained from joining the fighting. On one occasion, when his company ran out of wadding for its rifles, Caldwell ran into a nearby Presbyterian Church, scooped up as many Watts hymnals as he could carry, and distributed them to the troops, shouting "put Watts into them, boys."[19] Caldwell and his

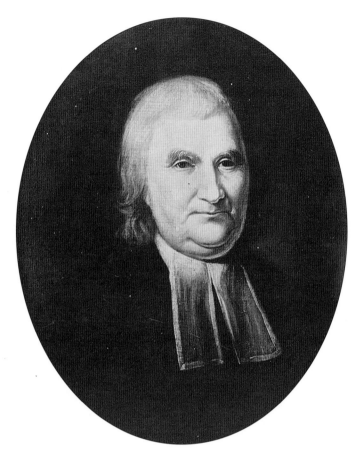

John Witherspoon.
Photograph of portrait by Charles Willson Peale.
Prints and Photographs Division (LC-USZ62-10022).

Witherspoon was the prototype of the political parson during the Revolutionary War.

wife were both killed by British sympathizers before the war ended.

It would be difficult to count the number of ministers who served in civil capacities during the revolutionary period. Most committees of safety and correspondence had at one time or another clerical representation. Ministers served in state legislatures and constitutional conventions and at least three of them, the most famous being the Presbyterian colossus John Witherspoon (1723–1794), sat in the Continental Congress. Witherspoon, who, as president of Princeton, was accused of turning that institution into a "seminary of sedition," signed the Declaration of Independence and, during a six-year stint in Congress, served on over one hundred committees. At the close of the war, Witherspoon preached a sermon (December 11, 1783) which summarized the views of his ministerial brethren: "The separation of this country from Britain has been of God; for every step the British took to prevent seemed to accelerate it, which has generally been the case when men have undertaken to go in opposition to the course of Providence."[20]

What effect did the Revolutionary War have on the institutional life of the church? It did not, as has previously been noted, stop the course of religious revivals. But its influence was not altogether benign. Churches were damaged and destroyed—often maliciously—by marauding armies; services were suspended when ministers went off to war; and the militarization of society, it was claimed, lowered the moral tone of many congregations.

If religion was harmed by the war, the damage was uneven. The Philadelphia Baptist Association, for example, lost one half of its adult members between 1776 and 1781. Yet between 1776 and 1783 membership in the Charleston Baptist Association almost doubled. The war produced a schism among the Quakers. Although most Friends adhered, often at great personal and financial peril, to their traditional peace testimony, some of their brethren organized themselves as "Free Quakers" and fought for the patriot cause. The Anglicans suffered the most severe damage from the war. Many of their priests, bound by ordination oaths to support the King, could not bring themselves to approve American independence, with the result that they vacated more than half of the country's Anglican pulpits by war's end.[21] The Church's loss may have been the country's gain, however, for the flight of its priests may have spared the United States the travail of France, where more than half of the clergy refused to accept the French Revolution, forming a reactionary core which sustained malcontents and destabilized the nation's politics far into the future. The departure of the irreconcilable Anglicans assured that there would be no entrenched, enduring, religiously based opposition to the new American Republic.

Finally, the Revolution had an impact on American theology, specifically on millennialist expectations—the belief that, either before or after some unfathomable cataclysm, Christ would return and reign on earth in power and glory for a thousand years. Having intervened, as it was generally believed, to liberate America from British tyranny, God was thought by many to be primed for the more exalted project of ushering in the millennium on the liberated, republican soil of the United States. Even at the beginning of the war some ministers were persuaded that, with God's help, America might become "the principal Seat of the glorious Kingdom which Christ shall erect upon Earth in the latter Days" and the achievement of victory stimulated an outpouring of millennialist expectations.[22] The subject would be of interest only to religious specialists had not millennialism coincided with a groundswell of secular optimism about the future of America; together the two trends created the buoyant mood of the new nation that became so evident after Jefferson assumed the presidency in 1801.[23]

Jacob Duché offering the first prayer in Congress, September 7, 1774. Bottom pane of the Liberty Window, Christ Church, Philadelphia, after a painting by Harrison Tompkins Matteson, c. 1848. Courtesy of Christ Church, Philadelphia, and Deborah M. Gough, *Christ Church, Philadelphia* (University of Pennsylvania Press, 1995).

John Adams described the services in Carpenter's Hall on September 7, 1774: Duché "read several Prayers, in the established Form; and then read the Collect for the seventh day of September, which was the Thirty fifth Psalm . . . after this Mr. Duché, unexpected to every Body struck out into an extemporary Prayer, which filled the Bosom of every Man present. I must confess that I never heard a better Prayer or one so well pronounced . . . with such fervour, such Ardor, such Earnestness and Pathos, and in Language so elegant and sublime—for America, for the Congress, for The Province of Massachusetts Bay, and especially the Town of Boston. It has had an excellent Effect upon every Body here."

FOUR ✣

RELIGION AND THE CONGRESS
OF THE CONFEDERATION, 1774–89

The United States' first national government was the Continental-Confederation Congress, which functioned from 1774 to 1789, when it was replaced by the new federal government created by the Constitution. Congress, as it was called throughout its existence, resembled a conjurer. With little official power, a small and often absentee membership, and no permanent home, it defeated the world's greatest military power, concluded the most successful peace treaty in American history, survived severe economic turbulence, and devised a brilliant plan for settling the American West. Equally remarkable was the energy Congress invested in encouraging the practice of religion throughout the new nation, energy that far exceeded the amount expended by any subsequent American national government.

Perhaps only Cromwell's parliaments can compare to Congress in the number of deeply religious men in positions of national legislative leadership. Charles Thomson (1729–1804), the soul of Congress and the source of its institutional continuity as

its permanent secretary from 1774 to 1789, retired from public life to translate the Scriptures from Greek to English; the four-volume Bible that Thomson published in 1808 is admired by modern scholars for its accuracy and learning. John Dickinson (1732–1808), who, as the "Pennsylvania Farmer," was the colonies' premier political pamphleteer, and who, as a member of Congress in 1776, wrote the first draft of the Articles of Confederation, also retired from public life to devote himself to religious scholarship, writing commentaries on the Gospel of Matthew. So did Elias Boudinot (1740–1821), president of Congress, 1782–83, who tuned out "warm" debates on the floor to write his daughter long letters, praying that, through the blood of God's "too greatly despised Son," she should be "born again to the newness of Life." Resigning as director of the U.S. Mint in 1805, Boudinot wrote religious tracts such as *The Second Advent* (1815) and the next year became the first president of the American Bible Society. Henry Laurens (1724–1792), president of Congress, 1777–78, was "strict and exemplary" in the performance of his religious duties. He "read the scriptures diligently to his family" and "made all his children read them also. His family Bible contained in his own handwriting several of his remarks on passing providences." John Jay (1745–1829), Laurens' successor as president of Congress, 1778–79, and later first chief justice of the Supreme Court, was extolled for "the firmness, even fervor, of his religious conviction." When he retired from public life, he also became president of the American Bible Society (1821). Even the two congressmen who defected to the British were distinguished by their religious, if not their patriotic, ardor: John Joachim Zubly of Georgia (1724–1781) was a Presbyterian minister and Joseph Galloway of Pennsylvania, a major figure at the First Continental Congress, later published commentaries on Revelations, which he prescribed as a "pill for the infidel and atheist."[1]

That a deeply religious society should produce

Benjamin Franklin and Thomas Jefferson, legends for the Great Seal of the United States, 1776. Thomas Jefferson Papers, Manuscript Division (LCMS-27748-181 & LCMS-27748-182).

On July 4, 1776, Congress appointed a committee of Benjamin Franklin, Thomas Jefferson, and John Adams "to bring in a device for a seal for the United States of America." By August 13, the members had prepared their recommendations. Adams suggested a subject from classical antiquity, Hercules. Franklin's proposal, an adaptation of the story in Exodus of the parting of the Red Sea, is in his handwriting on the lower slip of paper, preserved in the Jefferson Papers. Jefferson first recommended the "Children of Israel in the Wilderness, led by a Cloud by Day, and a Pillar of Fire by night, and on the other Side Hengist and Horsa, the Saxon Chiefs from whom We claim the Honour of being descended." He then embraced Franklin's proposal and rewrote it, as the description in his hand on the top slip demonstrates. Jefferson's revision of Franklin's proposal was presented by the committee to Congress on August 20. It was tabled and not revived.

deeply religious leaders is no surprise, but the power of religion in revolutionary America was also displayed in the legislative activities of those described as theological liberals. Consider the actions of Franklin and Jefferson when they were appointed in July 1776 to a committee to devise a seal for the United States. Both men suggested a familiar Old Testament episode that was a transparent allegory for America's ordeal, the account in the book of Exodus of God's intervening to save the people of Israel by drowning Pharoah (George III) and his pursuing armies in the Red Sea. In the opinion of these two torchbearers of the Enlightenment, nothing less than the story of a biblical miracle would be an appropriate emblem for their confessing countrymen.

At its initial meeting, in September 1774, Congress made it a first order of business to find a Gospel minister to open its sessions with prayer. Selected was the Reverend Jacob Duché (1738–1798), a Philadelphia Anglican priest, whose piety and zeal pleased and, ultimately, deceived the members when he defected to the British in 1777. Duché ministered to Congress in an unofficial capacity until he was elected that body's first chaplain on July 9, 1776.

Duché knew the piety of his congressional audience and saluted it in a sermon delivered to the delegates in July 1775. "Go on, ye chosen band of Christians," he urged the members.[2] Go on they did, frequently acting like a committee of lay ministers, preaching to the people of the United States as a national congregation, urging them to confess their sins, to repent, and to bear fruits that befit repentance.

Congress's first charge to its constituents was its resolution of June 12, 1775, setting a national day of "public humiliation, fasting and prayer" five

Proposed Great Seal of the United States: "Rebellion to Tyrants is Obedience to God." Drawing by Benson J. Lossing, for *Harper's New Monthly Magazine*, July 1856, reproduced in Richard S. Patterson and Richardson Dougall, *The Eagle and the Shield* (Washington, D.C., 1976). General Collections.

An artist's rendering of the Franklin-Jefferson proposal for the Great Seal of the United States.

**In Congress, Saturday, March 16, 1776
[Congressional Fast Day Proclamation].
Broadside Collection,
Rare Book and Special Collections Division.**

Congress sets Friday, May 17, as a "day of Humiliation, Fasting and Prayer" throughout the colonies. This document is characteristic of the numerous fast and thanksgiving day proclamations issued by Congress throughout the Revolutionary War. All contained Christian language, though not in every case a specific invocation of the "merits and mediation of Jesus Christ." Note that Massachusetts ordered that a "suitable Number" of these proclamations be printed "in order that each of the religious Assemblies in this Colony, may be furnished with a Copy of the same" and added the motto "God Save This People" as a substitute for "God Save the King."

weeks later on July 20.[3] This resolution was communicated to state authorities, then to the churches, establishing a channel that Congress used repeatedly to relay political information to the nation's citizens. On May 8, 1778, for example, Congress issued an assessment of the country's political and military situation which it ordered to be read by "ministers of the gospel of all denominations . . . immediately after divine services." By participating in this process the clergy became political auxiliaries of Congress. The May 8 address, which was duly read in the churches, was a characteristic congressional state paper because of its repeated references to religion: "our dependence was not upon man," Congress asserted, "it was upon Him who hath commanded us to love our enemies, and to render good for evil"; our success has been "so peculiarly marked, almost by direct interposition of Providence, that not to feel and acknowledge his protection would be the height of impious ingratitude."[4]

The "Continental fast" of July 20 did not disappoint those like John Adams, who predicted that "Millions will be on their Knees at once before their great Creator, imploring His Forgiveness and Blessing, His Smiles on American Councils and Arms."[5] On the appointed day, Congress attended services and heard sermons in the morning at Duché's Anglican Church and in the afternoon at Francis Alison's Presbyterian meeting, being careful, as it was throughout the war, not to patronize exclusively any one denomination, lest it be accused of religious favoritism. Later, Congress worshipped en masse at Philadelphia's "Roman Chapel," July 4, 1779, and at the "Dutch Lutheran Church," October 24, 1781. In an additional effort to appear evenhanded in religious matters, Congress, after the Duché debacle, appointed joint chaplains of different denominations.

Certain phrases in Congress's proclamation of June 12, setting the July 20 fast—God's "desolating judgments," "confess and deplore our many sins," "beseech him to forgive our iniquities," "implore his merciful interposition for our deliverance"—have tipped scholars off to the fact that Congress had adopted and was expounding a venerable religious doctrine called "covenant theology."[6] As old as the Reformation itself, this doctrine was embraced by all of the major Protestant groups who settled America, although it has become known as one of the signature statements of the New England Puritans.

Covenant theology was simplicity itself. It held that God had condescended to bind himself to human beings by what amounted to a legal agreement—a covenant—to reward their faithfulness and punish their sins. Preachers explained that, as parties to a covenant, "a people should be prosperous or afflicted, according as their general Obedience or Disobedience thereto appears."[7] God might visit a sinful people with natural afflictions—floods, droughts, epidemics—or political ones—oppression, rebellions, wars. Although secular men might ascribe the controversy with the mother country to a conspiracy of rapacious British politicians, religious Americans knew better. As a preacher explained, "in seasons of great difficulty and distress we are apt to look too much to second causes, and to forget that whatever evil or calamity is brought upon us, the hand of the Lord is in it."[8]

This was precisely the message Duché delivered to Congress in his sermon of July 20, 1775. The conflict with the mother country, he admonished the members, was God's doing, a "national punishment" for "national guilt."[9] There was no reason to despair, however, for God was as merciful as He was just, and He was always ready to let those with

whom He had covenanted regain His favor. This could be done by a step-by-step method that included acknowledgment of God's sovereignty and agency in human events (in pain as well as pleasure), confession of sin, repentance, and expectation of deliverance through God's mercy.

For ten years, from its first fast day proclamation of June 12, 1775 until its final thanksgiving proclamation of August 3, 1784, Congress adopted and preached to the American people the political theology of the national covenant, the belief that the war with Britain was God's punishment for America's sins and that national confession and repentance would reconcile Him to the country and cause Him to bare His mighty arm and smite the British. Congress was, obviously, recommending repentance as a military strategy, but no one objected, for covenant theology had legitimized this approach for generations. Although it would have preferred more concrete assistance from the political leadership, the American military did not disparage covenant theology. Congress's faith in its potency never flagged, however, and every year during the war it broadcast it to the people at least twice, once in a March fast day proclamation and once in an October thanksgiving proclamation.

Selections from various fast day proclamations show how Congress, guided by covenant theology, drew the roadmap for regaining God's favor. The first requirement was that the American people recognize God's "overruling Providence" (1776);[10] then they must acknowledge that the war and its attendant evils were God's chastisements for the nation's sins, it having pleased God "for the punishment of our manifold offenses, to permit the sword of war still to harrass our country" (1780);[11] next they must "confess and bewail our manifold sins and trespasses" and exhibit "sincere repentance and amendment of life [to] appease his righteous displeasure" (1776, 1781);[12] finally, they should look for deliverance, hoping "that it may please the Lord of Hosts, the God of Armies, to animate our officers and soldiers with invincible fortitude . . . and to crown the continental arms, by sea and land, with victory and success" (1776).[13]

Since collective, national sins were held to have provoked God to punish the country with war, Congress repeatedly entreated God to help produce a national reformation of religion. His power was sought in proclamations in 1776 to assure that "pure undefiled religion, may universally prevail";[14] in 1777, "to prosper the means of religion for the promotion and enlargement of that kingdom which consisteth 'in righteousness, peace and joy in the Holy Ghost'";[15] and in 1778 that Americans might be "a reformed and happy people."[16] The language of the congressional proclamations was unapologetically Christian; Congress specifically sought the intervention on the nation's behalf of Jesus Christ, praying God in 1776 "through the merits and mediation of Jesus Christ [to] obtain his pardon and forgiveness,"[17] and in 1777 inviting its fellow Americans to "join the penitent confession of their manifold sins . . . and their humble and earnest supplication that it may please God, through the merits of Jesus Christ, mercifully to forgive and blot them out of remembrance."[18]

The most eloquent congressional proclamation, one whose stylistic excellence does not suffer in comparison to the best state papers of the period, was composed for the American people on March 20, 1779, and sent out over the signature of John Jay. It is reprinted here to give the reader the flavor of the constant stream of Congress's political-theological manifestos:

that he [God] will grant the blessings of peace to all contending nations, freedom to those who are in bondage, and comfort to the afflicted: that he will diffuse useful knowledge, extend the influence of true religion, and give us that peace of mind which the world cannot give: that he will be our shield in the day of battle, our comforter in the hour of death, and our kind parent and merciful judge through time and through eternity.[19]

Although Congress's principal weapon in its campaign for a religious citizenry was exhortation, it took action when it could. John Dickinson, for example, inserted in an early draft of the Articles of Confederation the requirement that every American go to church; if "such person frequents regularly some place of religious worship on the Sabbath," Dickinson promised that his religious liberty would be protected.[20] Congress laid down the law for personnel under its control, particularly members of the armed forces. In the Articles of War, governing the conduct of the Continental Army, adopted on June 30, 1775, and revised and expanded on September 20, 1776, Congress devoted three of the four articles in the first section to the religious nurture of the troops.[21] In Article 2 it was "earnestly recommended to all officers and soldiers to attend divine services." Punishment was prescribed for those who behaved "indecently or irreverently" in churches, including courts-martial, fines, and imprisonments; chaplains who deserted their troops were to be court-martialed.

Congress particularly feared the navy as a source of moral corruption and demanded that skippers of American ships make their men behave. The first article in Rules for the Regulation of the Navy,

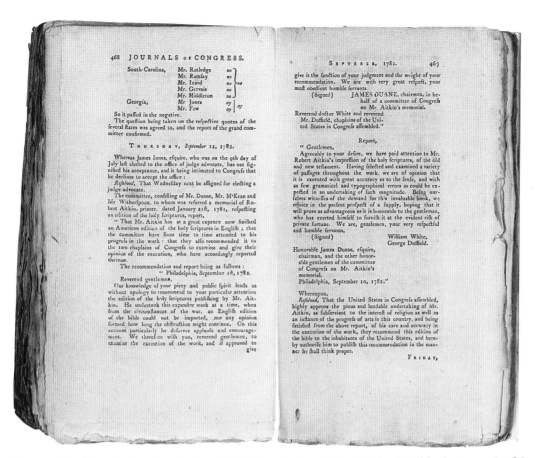

Congressional resolution, September 12, 1782, endorsing Robert Aitken's Bible, in *Journals of Congress,* **vol. VII, September 1782. Rare Book and Special Collections Division.**

Congress's Journals *for September 12, 1782, contains the testimony of its chaplains, William White and George Duffield, that Robert Aitken had executed his edition of the Bible with "great accuracy" and Congress's recommendation of Aitken's "edition of the Bible to the inhabitants of the United States." Authorized by Congress to "publish this recommendation in the manner he shall think proper," Aitken printed the chaplain's testimonial and the congressional recommendation, as seen here, as an imprimatur on the two pages following his title page, seen in the next illustration.*

adopted on November 28, 1775, ordered all commanders "to shew themselves a good example of honor and virtue to their officers and men and to be very vigilant . . . to discountenance and suppress all dissolute, immoral and disorderly practices." The second article required those same commanders "to take care, that divine services be performed twice a day on board, and a sermon preached on Sundays." Article 3 prescribed punishments for swearers and blasphemers: officers were to be fined and common sailors were to be forced "to wear a wooden collar or some other shameful badge of distinction."[22]

It is difficult to overemphasize Congress's concern for the spiritual condition of the armed forces, for the covenant mentality convinced it that irreligion in the ranks was, of all places, the most dangerous, for God might directly punish a backsliding military with defeat, extinguishing in the process American independence. Congress expressed its anxiety in its fast day proclamation of December 11,

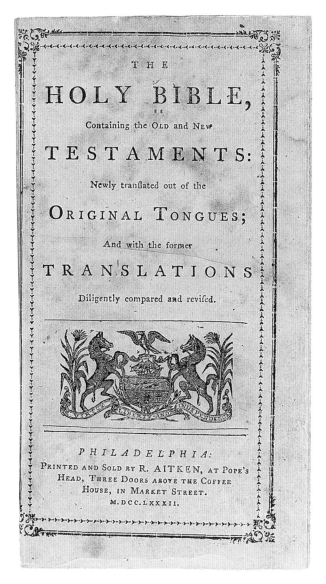

The Holy Bible, Containing the Old and New Testaments Newly translated out of the Original Tongues; And with the former Translations Diligently compared and revised **(Philadelphia: Printed and Sold by R. Aitken, 1782). Rare Book and Special Collections Division.**

Robert Aitken's Bible, which was recommended to the people of the United States by the Confederation Congress on September 12, 1782.

1776, recommending "in the most earnest manner" to "officers civil and military under them, the exercise of repentance and reformation; and further, require of them the strict observation of the articles of war, and particularly, that part of the said articles, which forbids profane swearing, and all immorality." [23]

An unfailing antidote to immorality was Bible reading. Hostilities, however, had interrupted the supply of Bibles from Great Britain, raising fears of a shortage of Scripture just when it was needed most. In the summer of 1777, three Presbyterian ministers warned Congress of this danger and urged it to arrange for a domestic printing of the Bible. Upon investigation, a committee of Congress discovered that it would be cheaper to import Bibles from continental Europe and made such a recommendation to the full Congress on September 11, 1777. Congress approved the recommendation on the same day, instructing its Committee of Commerce to import twenty thousand Bibles from "Scotland, Holland or elsewhere" but adjourned—the British were poised to take Philadelphia—without passing implementing legislation. [24]

The issue of the Bible supply was raised again in Congress in 1780 when it was moved that the states be requested "to procure one or more new and correct editions of the Old and New Testaments to be published." The committee to whom this motion was referred was in due course charged with evaluating a petition (January 21, 1781) from a Philadelphia printer, Robert Aitken (1734–1802), that the national legislature officially sanction a publication of the Old and New Testament that he was preparing at his own expense. By September 1, 1782, Aitken's Bible was finished and Congress asked its chaplains—William White (1748–1836) and George Duffield (1732–1790)—for their opinion of it. Having received the chaplains' report on September 10 that Aitken had done his work with "great accuracy," Congress on September 12 passed the following resolution: "The United States in Congress assembled, highly approve the pious and laudable undertaking of Mr. Aitken, as subservient to the interest of religion . . . and being satisfied from the above report, of his care and accuracy in the execution of the work, they recommend this edition of the Bible to the inhabitants of the United States." Aitken's edition of the Scriptures, published under congressional patronage, appeared shortly thereafter. It was the first English language Bible published on the North American continent.[25]

A Congress that constantly exhorted its constituents to promote the spread of Christianity, to spare no efforts, as its fast day proclamation of March 19, 1782, urged, to see that the "religion of our Divine Redeemer . . . cover the earth as the waters cover the seas,"[26] could not be indifferent to the cause of Christ in the vast new territories—stretching from the Allegheny Mountains to the Mississippi River—acquired from Britain in the peace settlement of 1783. Accordingly, when Congress, in the spring of 1785, debated regulations for selling property in the new lands, it was moved that the central section in each township should be reserved for the support of schools and "the Section immediately adjoining the same to the northward, for the support of religion. The profits arising therefrom in both instances, to be applied for ever according to the will of the majority."[27] This proposal, which established religion in the traditional sense of granting state funding to a church that would be controlled by one denomination, attracted support, but was voted down on April 23, 1785.

Continuing to share the widespread concern about the corrupting influence of the frontier, Con-gress in the summer of 1787 revisited the issue of religion in the new territories and passed, July 13, 1787, the famous Northwest Ordinance. Article 3 of the Ordinance contained the following language: "Religion, Morality and knowledge being necessary to good government and the happiness of mankind, Schools and the means of education shall forever be encouraged."[28] Scholars have been puzzled that, having declared religion and morality indispensable to good government, Congress did not, like some states that had written similar declarations into their constitutions, give financial assistance to the churches in the West. Although rhetorical encouragement for religion was all that was possible on this occasion, Congress did, in a little noticed action two weeks later, offer financial support to a church. In response to a plea from Bishop John Ettwein (1721–1802), Congress voted, July 27, 1787, that ten thousand acres on the Muskingum River in the present state of Ohio "be set apart and the property thereof be vested in the Moravian Brethren . . . or a society of the said Brethren for civilizing the Indians and promoting Christianity."[29]

Under what authority did Congress conduct its wide-ranging activities in religion, its sermonizing the country, its sponsoring a Bible, its appointing chaplains for civilian and military duty, its criminalizing non-Christian activity in the armed forces, its granting public land to promote Christianity? The Articles of Confederation gave Congress so little power that, at times, it almost ceased to function. Nowhere in those circumscribed powers was there any mention of the power to legislate on religion. Yet, aside from complaints about granting land for religious purposes in the abortive Ordinance of April 23, 1785, no voices were raised by a notoriously jealous citizenry about Congress's broad program to promote religion. It appears that both the politicians and the public held an unarticulated conviction that it was the duty of the national government to support religion, that it had an inherent power to do so, as long as it acted in a nonsectarian way without appropriating public money. What other body, after all, was capable of convincing a dispersed people that "a spirit of universal reformation among all ranks and degrees of our citizens," would, as Congress declared on March 19, 1782, "make us a holy, that so we may be a happy people?"[30] This conviction—that holiness was a prerequisite for secular happiness, that religion was, in the words of the Northwest Ordinance, "necessary to good government and the happiness of mankind"—was not the least of the Confederation's legacies to the new republican era that began with Washington's inauguration in 1789.

FIVE ✼

RELIGION AND THE STATE GOVERNMENTS

That holiness was necessary for secular happiness was not an idea that grew, like some exotic plant, only in the environs of Congress. It was the common conviction of the American people when independence forced them, in 1776, to establish governments in each of the former colonies. The relationship of church to state became an issue in many of the new governments, for if "pure, undefiled religion" was in the public interest, as Congress constantly assured the American people that it was, it seemed to follow that the new state governments must take responsibility for the condition of religion in their jurisdictions, must support religion financially, if necessary, so that it could be the rock on which the public welfare rested. As the debate about the relationship between religion and civil society developed in the state legislatures and constitutional conventions, it focused not so much on the large question of a whole people's obedience to a national covenant with God—this was Congress's concern—as on the more specific issues of reli-

gion's ability to produce the special kinds of citizens needed to make republican government work and its role in building in the population that basic degree of social responsibility necessary for a civilized existence.

To many people, a church-state partnership was the only way to produce a virtuous society, yet this goal seemed to collide with another equally powerful revolutionary goal—the free exercise of religion (as the First Amendment later phrased it). The first objective required state action in, the second seemed to dictate state retraction from, the religious sphere. The solution to the dilemma of how the state could use religion without abusing it, of how it could support religion without subverting religious liberty, was sought with differing results in Virginia, Massachusetts, and elsewhere. The issue created an intense debate about the possibility of a constructive engagement of government and religion which is often neglected in popular histories of the period. These leave the impression that the Declaration of Independence loosed a

59

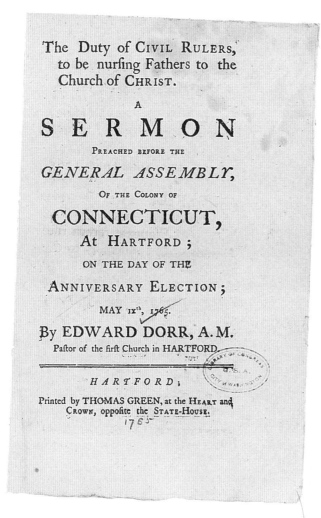

The Duty of CIVIL RULERS, to be nursing Fathers to the Church of CHRIST.

A

SERMON

PREACHED BEFORE THE

GENERAL ASSEMBLY,

OF THE COLONY OF

CONNECTICUT,

At HARTFORD;

ON THE DAY OF THE

ANNIVERSARY ELECTION;

MAY ix^th, 1765.

By EDWARD DORR, A.M.

Pastor of the first Church in HARTFORD.

HARTFORD;

Printed by THOMAS GREEN, at the HEART and CROWN, opposite the STATE-HOUSE.

1765

Edward Dorr, *The Duty of Civil Rulers, to be nursing Fathers to the Church of Christ* (Hartford, Connecticut, 1765). American Imprints, Rare Book and Special Collections Division.

The belief that the state, described by the Old Testament metaphor, nursing father, should support the church had existed for centuries in western Europe and was deeply rooted in the mentality and traditions of Anglicans, Congregationalists, and Presbyterians. The belief persisted after independence and played a major role in the debates over church-state relations in the new republic.

widespread loathing in the new nation for state involvement with the churches, leading to the swift and decisive banishment of the government from the religious realm.

Debate over religion was muted in those states which, as colonies, refrained from establishing a church (granting one denomination exclusive financial and legal privileges). In these jurisdictions—Rhode Island, New Jersey, Pennsylvania, and Delaware—the citizens saw little reason to tamper with arrangements that had served them well. Discord arose in the other states—the majority of the new nation—where religion had been established in the colonial period: in New England, where Congregationalism reigned, and in Maryland and the states to the south, where the Church of England prevailed. Before 1776, establishments in these states had tried in various degrees to accommodate dissenting denominations—in New England, for example, dissenters were granted exemptions from religious taxation—but beneficiaries of these measures were not happy with their subordinate situation and hoped to use the rebellion against Great Britain as the occasion for ending their second class status. Supporters of the established churches refused, however, to renounce the idea that a judicious measure of state support for religion was good public policy, contending that independence posed challenges that made the practice more necessary than ever.

Advocates of state-supported religion argued their case with an Old Testament metaphor whose use in English political discourse dated back to Elizabethan times. Governments in the United States, they argued, must be "nursing fathers" of the church (Isaiah 49:23). This concept was embraced and incorporated in authoritative pronouncements of many of America's churches. It appeared in Bishop Jewel's *An apologie . . . in defence of the Church of*

England (1562), in the Presbyterians' Westminster Confession, and in the Cambridge Platform of 1648, the "creed" of New England Congregationalism.

The primary duty of a nursing father-magistrate in the seventeenth century was to enforce religious uniformity by extinguishing error, as authorities in New England and Virginia tried to do in the 1660s. By sanctioning religious dissent, the Toleration Act of 1689 caused the definition of the task of political authorities, as nursing fathers of the church, to change to one of promoting the general welfare of religion, principally by providing financial support. Thus, in 1704, an Anglican missionary in New Jersey praised the church's benefactor, Governor Francis Nicholson (1655–1728), for being a "true son or rather Nursing Father of her in America," while, the next year, two New York Anglican missionaries extolled their governor, Lord Cornbury (1661–1723), "for his eminent care and protection of us; he is truly our Nursing Father."[1] In New England, the term nursing father was in constant use, as, for example, in a pamphlet written in 1744 by Elisha Williams (1694–1755), a former president of Yale, who claimed that "the Civil Authority of a State are obliged to take Care for the Support of Religion, or in other words, of Schools and the Gospel Ministry, in order to their approving themselves Nursing Fathers (as, I suppose, every Body will own, and therefore I shall not spend any time proving it)."[2] Sermons were preached like Edward Dorr's *The Duty of Civil Rulers, to be nursing Fathers to the Church of Christ* (Hartford, 1765) and, in 1775, Massachusetts complained that British officials had defaulted on their traditional obligation to the colonial church: "those who should be Nursing Fathers became its Persecutors."[3]

Long conditioned to think that the state should nurture the church, many Americans would have agreed with Irenaeus, writing in a Massachusetts newspaper, March 9, 1780, that "a very respectable part of this Commonwealth look upon it as a duty which God requires of Legislators, that they make suitable provision for the support of public worship and teachers of religion. And not only so, but they esteem it as one of their most sacred and invaluable rights."[4] Similar sentiments were expressed by the citizens of Amherst County, Virginia, on November 27, 1783, when they petitioned their representatives not to ignore the "Important Business" of supporting religion or "think it beneath your Dignity to become Nursing Fathers of the Church."[5] As late as 1826 the term "nursing fathers" of the church can be found in the promotional literature of American home missionary societies.

Those arguing, in the years following independence, that the state should succor the church believed that the high level of public rectitude required for the successful establishment of republican government made their case for them. Republican government was, above all, self-government and self-government placed higher demands on the average citizen than any other polity. The citizens of Surry County, Virginia, explained why this was so in a petition to the General Assembly on December 1, 1784. Calling religion the "great Cement of civil society" and arguing that it was a "position coeval with the first rudiments of political union that religion has ever been found essential to the prosperity of civil government," the petitioners explained that in America "where liberty flourishes in its most luxuriant state . . . where much is left to [the peoples'] discretion, much to their caprice; the aid of religion will be more necessary and its influence more decisive, than in the Monarchies of Europe where the Governments have more energy and the subjects less liberty."[6]

In Europe, the responsibilities of citizenship were low, because authoritarian states took care of everything. In the new American republics, they were high and required a broad civic consciousness that the Founding generation called virtue. Virtue was a concept of classical antiquity that shared so many characteristics with Christianity—selfless service, honesty, simplicity—that the revolutionary generation regularly conflated it with Christian morality and assumed that it was best promoted by Christianity. The following syllogism imprinted itself so strongly on the minds of the Founders that it became a cliché: religion promoted virtue; virtue promoted republicanism; religion promoted, and was indispensable for, republicanism. In the words of Benjamin Rush (1745–1813), Christianity was "the strong ground of republicanism . . . many of its precepts have for their objects republican liberty and equality as well as simplicity, integrity, and economy in government."[7] A Georgia newspaper editor conveyed the same message to his readers when he wrote that it "was evident, that without Religion there can be no virtue; and it is equally incontestible that without virtue, there can be no liberty. At least, it is allowed, on all hands, that a large republic, especially, can not subsist without virtue."[8]

Republican virtue had, for many of the Founders, a special connotation of participation in public service. They did not, of course, expect every citizen to be ready or able to drop the plow and save the republic but they did expect their fellow Americans, however humble their station, to be virtuous in the more modest sense of acting in socially responsible ways and they counted on religion to create a basic level of good behaviour in the body politic. In 1794 Timothy Dwight (1752–1817) addressed the issue of the role of religion in creating responsible citizenship by arguing that from Christianity's "moral and religious instructions, the cogent motives to duty, and the excitements to decent, amiable and useful conduct which it furnishes, it establishes, perhaps more than any single thing, good order, good morals and happiness public and private. It makes good men and good men must be good citizens."[9]

In mentioning the "cogent motives to duty" furnished by Christianity, Dwight was referring to what other writers called the "awful solemnity" of its supernational sanctions, hell fire for the wicked man, paradise for the saint. The Christian doctrine of the "future state of rewards and punishments," when internalized by believers, was considered by the revolutionary generation to be a far more effective source of acceptable social behavior than "human laws," which, according to the Boston Town Meeting, May 30, 1780, were but "feble barriers opposed to the uninformed lusts of Passions of Mankind."[10] "The belief of future state of rewards and punishments," wrote Irenaeus in 1780, was "absolutely necessary for the well being of civil society, . . . for we shall find that persons are often restrained from gross immoralities by the fear of future miseries, when civil penalties prove insufficient for that purpose."[11] Christianity, declared the preacher of the Connecticut Election Sermon in 1780, "defends the property and persons of each individual, by considerations of infinite moment, as it denounces indignation and wrath, tribulation and anguish, upon every soul of man that doeth evil."[12] The Christian system of behavioral incentives / disincentives seemed to be so essential for the maintenance of social order that several states—Pennsylvania (1776), Vermont (1777), South Carolina (1778), and Tennessee (1796)—prohibited individuals from voting or holding offices who denied

[7]

PART the First.

A DECLARATION of the RIGHTS of the Inhabitants of the Commonwealth of MASSACHUSETTS.

Art. I. ALL men are born free and equal, and have certain natural, essential, and unalienable rights; among which may be reckoned the right of enjoying and defending their lives and liberties; that of acquiring, possessing, and protecting property; in fine, that of seeking and obtaining their safety and happiness.

II. IT is the right as well as the duty of all men in society, publicly, and at stated seasons, to worship the SUPREME BEING, the great creator and preserver of the universe. And no subject shall be hurt, molested, or restrained, in his person, liberty, or estate, for worshiping GOD in the manner and season most agreeable to the dictates of his own conscience; or for his religious profession or sentiments; provided he doth not disturb the public peace, or obstruct others in their religious worship.

III. As the happiness of a people, and the good order and preservation of civil government, essentially depend upon piety, religion and morality; and as these cannot be generally diffused through a community, but by the institution of the public worship of GOD, and of public instructions in piety, religion and morality: Therefore, to promote their happiness, and to secure the good order and preservation of their government, the people of this Commonwealth have a right to invest their legislature with

[8]

with power to authorize and require, and the legislature shall, from time to time, authorize and require, the several towns, parishes, precincts, and other bodies politic, or religious societies, to make suitable provision, at their own expence, for the institution of the public worship of GOD, and for the support and maintenance of public protestant teachers of piety, religion and morality, in all cases where such provision shall not be made voluntarily.

AND the people of this Commonwealth have also a right to, and do, invest their legislature with authority to enjoin upon all the subjects an attendance upon the instructions of the public teachers aforesaid, at stated times and seasons, if there be any on whose instructions they can conscientiously and conveniently attend.

PROVIDED notwithstanding, that the several towns, parishes, precincts, and other bodies-politic, or religious societies, shall, at all times, have the exclusive right of electing their public teachers, and of contracting with them for their support and maintenance.

AND all monies paid by the subject to the support of public worship, and of the public teachers aforesaid, shall, if he require it, be uniformly applied to the support of the public teacher or teachers of his own religious sect or denomination, provided there be any on whose instructions he attends; otherwise it may be paid towards the support of the teacher or teachers of the parish or precinct in which the said monies are raised.

AND every denomination of christians, demeaning themselves peaceably, and as good subjects of the Commonwealth, shall be equally under the protection

A Declaration of the Rights of the Inhabitants of the Commonwealth of Massachusetts.
[Massachusetts Constitution or Frame of Government, 1780].
American Imprints, Rare Book and Special Collections Division.

The third article of the Declaration of Rights of the Massachusetts Constitution of 1780 contained an explicit statement of the ancient conviction that religion was necessary for the public welfare and empowered the state legislature to compel subordinate jurisdictions to provide financial support for "the public worship of GOD, and for the support and maintenance of public protestant teachers of piety, religion and morality." The third article was one of the famous pronouncements of the revolutionary era and found its way into official documents in other states, as, for example, the Maryland Act to lay a general tax for the support of the ministers of the gospel of all societies of christians within this state (see p. 64).

the reality of a future state of rewards and punishments.

Christianity's value in supporting republican government seemed to be so obvious that Americans, as they established the first state constitutions, filled the newspapers and covered legislators' desks with articles and petitions about its importance.

"True religion," said the citizens of Surry County, Virginia, in 1785, "is most friendly to social and political Happiness. That a conscientious regard to the approbation of Almighty God lays the most effectual restraint on the vicious passions of Mankind, affords the most powerful incentive to the faithful Discharge of every sacred Duty and is consequently

By THE **HOUSE** OF **DELEGATES,**
JANUARY 12, 1785.

RESOLVED, *That the Bill to lay a general tax for the support of the ministers of the gospel of all societies of christians within this state, be referred and taken into considera-tion on the fifth day of the next session of assembly; and that the said bill be published in the Maryland Gazette, and Baltimore news-papers, and one thousand copies thereof in hand-bills, and sent to the several counties for the information of our constituents.*
By order, W. HARWOOD, clk.

An ACT to lay a general tax for the support of the ministers of the gospel of all societies of christians within this state.

WHEREAS the happiness of a people, and the good order and preserva-tion of civil government, essentially depend upon morality, religion, and piety, and these cannot be generally diffused through a community but by the public worship of Almighty God; and whereas our ancestors, the early settlers and respectable founders of this state, declaring " that matters concerning religion ought in the first place to be taken into consideration, countenanced, and encouraged, as being acceptable to God, and the best way and means of obtaining his mercy and blessing upon a people and country," did frame and establish sundry laws for the sup-port of religion, some of which, at the great æra of our independence, were, by the Bill of Rights, declared inconsistent with that religious liberty which was intended as the basis of our future government, but, at the same time, with an express pro-vision, that future legislators should pay a due regard to the essential concerns of reli-gion and piety, and, " at their discretion, lay a general and equal tax for the support of the christian religion,"

II. Be it enacted, *by the General Assembly of Maryland,* That every taxable inhabi-tant within this state shall annually, on or before the first day of August, pay unto the sheriff of his county the sum of ——— shillings current money; and if any taxable shall neglect or refuse to pay the same on or before the time aforesaid, it shall be law-ful for the sheriffs of the several counties, and they are hereby authorised and required, at any time after the first day of August annually, and within three months thereafter, to collect from every such taxable inhabitant the said sum of ——— shillings current money, by execution of the person, or by distress and sale (at auction after five days notice) of the goods or chattels of the person chargeable by this law with payment thereof; and the said sheriffs are hereby required, before the first day of November annually, to pay the money by them received or collected, or which by law they ought to have received and collected, to the person or persons entitled by this law to receive the same (after retaining five per cent. on such money for the receipt or collec-tion thereof); and if any sheriff shall not make payment according to the directions of this act, he shall forfeit, if suit be brought against him only, double the money which such sheriff ought to have received and collected, to be recovered by those who are entitled by this act to receive the same, with costs, by action on the case founded on this act, in which it shall be sufficient for the plaintiff to allege, that the defen-dant has received to the plaintiff's use the sum of money claimed by him, whereby the plaintiff's action accrued according to the form of this act, without setting forth the special matter; or the person entitled to receive from such sheriff may sue and re-cover on the sheriff's bond against him and his securities the money which such sheriff ought to have received and collected, with interest thereon from the time the money became payable; and every sheriff, on information that any inhabitant of his county is about to abscond or remove his effects from the place of his residence, may and shall, at any time between the first day of March and the twentieth day of October yearly, apply himself to some justice of his county, and, on oath or affirmation thereof made by the sheriff, or some other credible person (which oath or affirmation the said justice shall administer, and return to the next county court) such justice shall issue his warrant, and thereby authorise and direct such sheriff to execute such inhabitant or his goods or effects, and such sheriff shall make execution therefor without any for

[Maryland] House of Delegates, *An Act to lay a general tax for the support of the ministers of the gospel of all soci-eties of christians within this state.* **January 12, 1785. Broadside. Rare Book and Special Collections Division.**

The Maryland House printed this general assessment act as a broadside and, in January 1785, submitted it to the people of the state to solicit their opinion on the propriety of a general religious tax. Note that the first line of the act, beginning with "whereas," quotes Article 3 of the Massachusetts Constitution of 1780, re-versing the order of the nouns "morality," "religion," and "piety."

the most solid Basis of private and public Virtue is a truth which has in some measure been acknowl-edged at every Period of Time and in every corner of the Globe. It is a Truth sanctioned by the reason and experience of ages."[13]

"Mankind," claimed a writer in the *Virginia In-dependent Chronicle* in 1784, "have, generally speak-ing, enacted laws to restrain and punish enormities, to countenance virtue and discourage vice: yet the most approved and wisest legislators in all ages, in order to give efficacy to their civil institutions, have found it necessary to call in the aid of religion; and in no form of government whatever has the influ-ence of religious principles been found so requisite as in that of a republic."[14]

Expressing the view from Massachusetts, Su-preme Court Justice Joseph Story (1779–1845) later wrote that the "promulgation of the great doc-trines of religion, the being, and attributes, and providence of one Almighty God; the responsibility to him for all our actions, founded upon moral free-dom and accountability; a future state of rewards and punishments; the cultivation of all the personal, social, and benevolent virtues—these can never be matters of indifference in any well-ordered commu-nity. It is, indeed, difficult to conceive how any civi-lized society can well exist without them."[15]

The people of Lunenburg County, Virginia, summarized the sentiments of many Americans in November 1779, when they informed their repre-sentatives in the General Assembly that they had the right to establish Christianity on "Principles of Public Utility," because religion was "the best means of promoting Virtue, Peace and Prosperity."[16] From rural Virginia to Boston "Americans of the founding generation," as a recent scholar has ob-served, "rallied to the cause of religious faith."[17]

Public pressure for state support of religion animated legislators in most of the colonies that had supported colonial establishments. The Georgia Constitution of 1777 permitted taxation on behalf of religion. Declaring that Christianity's "regular establishment and support is among the most important objects of legislative determination," the state assembly in 1785 passed a law that allowed the imposition of religious taxes, although the statute does not appear to have been implemented.[18] The South Carolina Constitution of 1778 declared "the Christian Protestant religion shall be deemed, and is hereby constituted and declared to be, the established religion of the state."[19] In Maryland, the new state constitution of 1776 gave the legislature power to "lay a general and equal tax for the support of the Christian religion." In 1784, the House and Senate availed themselves of this power to pass a law laying a general religious tax, which they submitted to a popular referendum. The preamble to this statute repeated word for word the famous third article of the Massachusetts Constitution of 1780: "the happiness of a people, and the good order and preservation of civil government, essentially depend upon morality, religion and piety," reversing only the order of the last three nouns.[20]

It was, in fact, in Massachusetts and her New England neighbors and in Virginia, where the most firmly entrenched colonial establishments existed and where the "nursing fathers" tradition was the strongest, that the most determined efforts were made, after 1776, to establish tax-supported religion. Independence, however, had changed public sentiment in these areas and large numbers of people now resisted the restoration of an old style religious establishment. Dissenters from the old established churches, who had taken up arms to fight for freedom from British oppression, would no longer tolerate religious discrimination by their fellow citi-

zens. "Political equality," declared Presbyterians in Virginia, "is the undoubted Privelege of every Christian in the Federal Union," a "reward for the common blood and Treasure so freely spent by all."[21] Amen, asserted other erstwhile dissenters like the Maryland Catholic statesman, Charles Carroll (1737–1832), who declared that "freedom and Independence, acquired by the united efforts and cemented with the mingled blood of Protestant and Catholic fellow citizens shall be equally enjoyed by all."[22]

Confronted by these irresistible claims, legislators striving to support the churches devised what might be called religious equal opportunity laws, laying a general religious tax but permitting each citizen to pay the levy to the church of his choice. "Nothingarians" could designate their taxes for public education; "Jews and Turks" might be granted exemptions. These general assessment laws, as they were called, did not, in the opinion of their supporters, violate the clauses in the state constitutions guaranteeing religious liberty because, under their terms, the state did not coerce beliefs or religious practices; citizens were free to believe anything or nothing. "That the Legislature," declared a Virginia petition of 1785, "should provide for the support of an Institution so beneficial to Society as the Christian religion appears to us highly reasonable; and when no violation is offered to the Rights of private Judgement, but Men are left as free as Air in the Choice of their own Religion, we own ourselves at a loss to conceive on what Principles such Provision can be opposed . . . We can not conceive that the assessment which we contend for is in any respect opposed to the Bill of Rights because it grants no exclusive Privileges, it gives no Preference to any Society or Societys of Christians."[23] Here, then, was the solution that the states devised for the problem

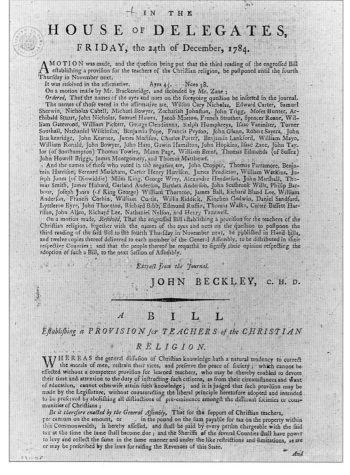

[Patrick Henry], *A Bill Establishing a Provision for Teachers of the Christian Religion.*
[Virginia] House of Delegates, December 24, 1784.
Broadside. Papers of George Washington,
Manuscript Division (LCMS-44693-177).

This broadside contains the opening sections of Patrick Henry's general assessment bill, one similar to those passed in the New England states; it laid a tax for the support of religion but permitted individuals to earmark their taxes for the churches of their choice. At the top of the broadside are the results of a vote, December 24, 1784, in the Virginia General Assembly to postpone consideration of the bill until the fall 1785 session of the legislature. Postponing the bill allowed opponents to mobilize and defeat it. Leading the forces for postponement was James Madison. Voting against postponement and, therefore, in support of a general assessment tax for religion was the future chief justice of the United States, John Marshall.

of supporting religion while not subverting the individual's right to free exercise thereof: general assessment laws.

Although general assessment laws were enacted in Massachusetts, Connecticut, and New Hampshire, and passed by both houses in Maryland and Georgia, scholars and jurists, in seeking to describe the emerging sentiment in the new American republic about the relationship between church and state, have focused on the one state in which efforts to pass a general assessment plan failed—the Commonwealth of Virginia. In Virginia, there was broad support for non-discriminatory state funding of religion. Legislation mandating this objective, Patrick Henry's "Bill Establishing a Provision for Teachers of the Christian Religion," was introduced into the General Assembly by the great orator in the fall of 1784. Henry's bill led off with what had become the conventional observation that "the general diffusion of Christian knowledge hath a natural tendency to correct the morals of men, restrain their vices, and preserve the peace of society"; it then proposed to lay a general tax which citizens could pay to the church of their choice or to a fund supporting public education in the commonwealth.[24] Henry's bill was supported by many of Virginia's giants; John Marshall (1755–1835), Richard Henry Lee (1732–1794), and George Washington (1732–1799), who wrote George Mason (1725–1792) on October 3, 1785, that he saw nothing wrong with requiring people to "pay towards the support of that which they profess."[25] The bill passed one reading in the House, 47–32; at the last minute, opponents prevented its enactment by neutralizing the legislative wizardry of Patrick Henry (1736–1799)—they elected him governor, November 17, 1784. The bill was then postponed, permitting the opposition to mobilize against it.

The bill's sponsor, Patrick Henry.

Patrick Henry. Stipple engraving by Leney, (detail) after Thomas Sully, 1817. Prints and Photographs Division (LC-USZ62-4907).

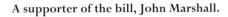

A supporter of the bill, John Marshall.

John Marshall. Engraving by Charles Balthazar Julien Fevret de Saint-Memin, 1808. Prints and Photographs Division (LC-USZ62-54940).

The mastermind of the opposition, James Madison.

James Madison. Miniature portrait by Charles Willson Peale, 1783. Rare Book and Special Collections Division (LC-USZC4-5310).

The principal adversaries of general assessment were an odd couple, acting from conflicting motives: evangelical Baptists and secular-minded civil libertarians. Virginia's Presbyterians, though committed evangelicals, vacillated. Historically, Presbyterians had subscribed to the nursing father model of church-state relations. The version of the Westminster Confession that they adopted in 1788 contained the phrase. Their principal spokesman, John Witherspoon, asserted that since "true religion is the best and most effectual way of making a virtuous and regular people," the magistrate, whose role was "something like that of a parent," was entitled to "make public provision for the worship of God."[26] In a petition to the General Assembly, November 12, 1784, the Hanover Presbytery adopted Witherspoon's and the denomination's traditional position that "it is absolutely necessary to the existence and welfare of every political combination of men in society to have the support of religion and its solemn institutions as affecting the conduct of rational beings more than human laws can possibly do. On this account it is wise policy of Legislators to seek its alliance and solicit its aid in a civil view . . . for inculcating the great fundamental principles . . . without which society could not easily exist." Soon after this petition was submitted, the bulk of Virginia's Presbyterians swung over into opposition to state support of religion—possibly, some have said, because of widespread aversion to new taxes of any kind—although none repudiated their Hanover brethrens' conviction that Christianity was the "Cement of the social union," or, in the words of Francis Alison (1705–1779), another major Presbyterian spokesman, "the cement of a civil constitution."[27]

The Baptists in Virginia and Massachusetts never wavered from their position that it was an abomination for the church to take financial assistance from the state. This was a fundamental Baptist principle,

written in much blood, about which there had never been any compromise. The magistrate, a Baptist leader asserted in 1611, "is not by virtue of his office to meddle with religion . . . for Christ only is king and lawgiver of the church."[28] Every Baptist argument in the 1780s was drawn from denominational testimony at least as old: since Christ's kingdom was not of this world, it could not be bankrolled by the state; since salvation was freely given, it could not be paid for by politicians.

American Baptists, on the other hand, were prepared to give the state wide latitude in offering non-discriminatory, non-financial assistance to religion in general. Isaac Backus, the Baptist intellectual spokesman, wrote in 1768 that there should be a "sweet harmony" between church and state, while other Baptist leaders welcomed "those friendly aids to the cause of our holy religion which may justly be expected from our political fathers."[29] Among the friendly aids the Baptists were prepared to receive were laws to preserve the sanctity of the sabbath, laws to compel citizens to attend church, and laws to impose Christian morality on society. "They think," a committee of "several Baptists Associations" in Virginia informed the General Assembly in August 1785, that the "Legislature will have sufficiently done its part in favour of Christianity when adequate provision is made for supporting those Laws of Morality, which are necessary for private and public happiness and of which it seems more properly the Guardian than of the peculiarities of the Christian Church."[30] With some exceptions like John Leland (1754–1841), the Baptists also supported the test acts, adopted by twelve of the thirteen revolutionary state governments, that permitted Christians and, in a few places, only Protestants, to hold public office. The most restrictive of these acts, which required office holders to profess a belief in the divine inspiration of the Old and

Rev. Isaac Backus, AM.
Portrait by unidentified artist, undated.
Trask Library, Andover Newton Theological School,
Newton Centre, Massachusetts.

Leader of the New England Separate Baptists and one of the great figures in the history of the Baptist Church in America, Backus was an implacable opponent of state financial support to churches.

New Testaments, were passed in Pennsylvania and Delaware, states where Baptists had a strong presence.

Baptist leaders also explicitly and publicly agreed with advocates of general assessment that religion was necessary for the health of civil society. Consider an exchange in 1778 between Isaac Backus and the Reverend Phillips Payson (1736–1801), a pillar of the Congregational establishment. In his Election Sermon before the Massachusetts legislature, Payson made the usual argument that "the importance of religion to civil society and government is great indeed . . . the fear and reverence of God, and the terrors of eternity are the most powerful restraints upon the minds of men . . . let the restraint of religion once be broken down . . . and we might well defy all human wisdom and power to support and preserve order and government in the state."[31] Just so, replied Backus, for he was "as sensible of the importance of religion and the utility of it to human society as Mr. Payson is."[32] Backus specifically endorsed the famous formulation of the Massachusetts Constitution of 1780; it is "readily granted," he wrote in 1784, "that piety, religion and morality are essentially necessary for the good order of society."[33] A Congregational minister claimed to be mystified that Backus could concede these premises yet oppose the "conclusions naturally and necessarily following from them," that the state must support religion financially. On this point, Backus's ideas were "prodigiously obscure," carped another opponent.[34]

The Baptists may have seemed obscure because they took the paradoxical position that the best way for the state to support religion was to do nothing. History was their witness here, for as they read it, it taught that in all places at all times religion suffered from state support and flourished when totally divorced from government. History's lesson was laid out in the most popular (in terms of signatures) anti-assessment petition in Virginia: "Certain it is that the Holy Author of our Religion not only supported and maintained his Gospel in the world for several hundred years without the aid of Civil Power, but against all the Powers of the Earth. The excellent purity of its precepts and the unblamable behavior of its Ministers (with the divine Blessing) made its way through all Opposition. Nor was it the better for the Church when Constantine first established Christianity by human Laws. True, there was rest from persecution, but how soon over Run with Error, Superstition, and Immorality; how unlike were Ministers then, to what they were before, both in orthodoxy of principle and purity of Life."[35]

It was obvious, then, to the Baptists that assessment bills were "not adopted to promote true Piety but rather to destroy it."[36] The only way to invigorate religion was to let it make its own way. There was no need to worry, for "God is ever engaged to maintain his own worship" and, as the Hanover Presbyterians claimed, "Christianity as in the days of the Apostles would continue to prevail and flourish in the greatest purity, by its own native excellence and under the all-disposing providence of God."[37] All that was needed, the evangelical Christians believed, was to free Christianity from the secular powers and principalities and let converted ministers go to work. In the words of a widely circulated Virginia anti-assessment petition: "Let ministers manifest to the world 'that they are inwardly moved by the Holy Ghost to take up that Office,' that they seek the good of Mankind and not worldly Interest. Let their doctrines be scriptural and their Lives upright. Then shall Religion (if departed) speedily return."[38] The religion that returned would, of course, be that of a population that had experienced the new birth.

The Baptists, Presbyterians, and Methodists did not deny that the new birth brought social benefits, as their opponents peevishly conceded. To the average Virginia gentleman, the Baptists were "quite destroying pleasure in the country; for they encourage ardent Pray'r: strong and constant faith, and an intire Banishment of Gaming, Dancing, and Sabbath-Day Diversions." By imposing "gospel discipline" on their redeemed communities, the evangelicals raised the moral standards of their fellow communicants to a level of "seriousness" and strictness that, in the eyes of some gentry, threatened to put Virginia in a puritanical straitjacket. No doubt the Commonwealth would profit from a large harvest of sober, godly citizens and no doubt some evangelical preachers took considerable satisfaction in this development. But the evangelical ministers never forgot that their first priority was the salvation of souls; the creation of good citizens must always remain a by-product of that effort.[39]

The motives of James Madison and Thomas Jefferson (looking on from Europe) in rallying the evangelical forces to oppose Henry's bill and to effect the disestablishment of religion in Virginia have been subject to various interpretations. A recent scholar has made the provocative claim that they actually shared the agenda of their evangelical allies, hoping that by freeing the Commonwealth's churches from the corrupting embrace of the state they "would ignite a religious revival favorable to the cause of republican government."[40] Whether this thesis is credible depends on an estimate of the religious views of Madison and Jefferson in the 1780s, a subject which both men were reluctant to discuss, even privately.

Madison appears to have been more respectful, as a younger man, of religion than Jefferson. He apparently considered entering the ministry as an undergraduate at Princeton. He "affirmed some basic Calvinist tenets as late as 1778"[41] and among his

The dunking of David Barrow and Edward Mintz in the Nansemond River, 1778.
Oil painting by Sidney E. King, 1990. Virginia Baptist Historical Society, Richmond.

Barrow was the pastor of the Mill Swamp Baptist Church in the Portsmouth, Virginia, area. Baptists were the core of the opposition to Henry's general assessment bill. In Virginia they suffered persistent physical persecution from supporters of the Church of England, often in league with local authorities. Dunking, as a mockery of the Baptist practice of the immersion of believers, was meted out to "Anabaptists" as far back as the sixteenth century; some died during the ordeal.

James Madison, *A Memorial and Remonstrance*, [June 1785]. Manuscript Division (LCMS-31021-86).

This famous appeal for religious liberty was written by Madison in the summer of 1785 as a contribution to the grass roots campaign to defeat Henry's general assessment bill. The Memorial and Remonstrance was printed as a petition in multiple copies and circulated throughout Virginia. Signed by at least fifteen hundred citizens, it was submitted, along with scores of other petitions for and against the general assessment bill, to the October 1785 session of the Virginia General Assembly. The meticulous handwritten copy seen here may have been the printer's copy or it could have been executed by Madison as a kind of personal keepsake.

papers an early biographer found "minute and elaborate notes made by him on the Gospels and the Acts of the Apostles which evince a close and discriminating study of the sacred writings . . . as well as the whole field of theological literature."[42] Notes for a speech that he made against Henry's bill in December 1784 indicate that Madison shared the common view of religion's value for social and political stability. "True question not," Madison jotted, "Is Religion necessary? are Religious Establishments necessary for religion?"[43] In Madison's famous petition against Henry's bill, his *Memorial and Remonstrance against Religious Assessments*, published anonymously in July 1785, the burden of his argument was based on natural rights, especially the right of freedom of judgment in religion enshrined in the Virginia Declaration of Rights of 1776, which he had helped write. Yet, toward the end of the *Memorial and Remonstrance,* Madison extolled Christianity as a "precious gift," deplored the fate of those living under "the Dominion of false Religions," and regretted that religious establishments placed an "obstacle before the victorious progress of Truth."[44] These sentiments may have been concocted merely to please an evangelical audience, but they may also have represented Madison's real, though carefully concealed, views on religion.

For Jefferson in the 1770s and 1780s there was nothing whatsoever precious about Christianity. He was, at this stage of his life, a confirmed deist to whom religion was, or should be, nothing more than the best moral teachings of classical antiquity. He was prepared to concede that religion, in spite of itself, had some social value; it was, he wrote in his *Notes on the State of Virginia*, "sufficient to preserve peace and order."[45] But he wished to strip it of even this social function by establishing a system of secular public schools in Virginia in which, as he

Thomas Jefferson, *An Act for establishing Religious Freedom*, January 1786. Broadside Collection, Rare Book and Special Collections Division.

This act, which Jefferson directed to be inscribed on his tombstone as comparable in importance to the Declaration of Independence, does not, like Madison's Memorial and Remonstrance, *exist in a handwritten copy. The version shown here was printed in a broadside in London in 1786 by Dr. Richard Price, the great civil libertarian and friend of America, who wrote the introduction and made changes in the text.*

indicated in his *Bill for the More General Diffusion of Public Knowledge* (1778), the study of history, not the Bible, would be used to inculcate the virtue and morality necessary for a republican citizenry.

It was in this deistical, sectarian spirit that Jefferson wrote, in 1777, his *Bill for Establishing Religious Freedom*, a state paper that he put on a par with the Declaration of Independence. The bill, which proposed to liberate the mind from all forms of government control, especially from an officially imposed religion, abounds with famous phrases: "Almighty God hath created the mind free"; "our civil rights have no dependance on our religious opinions, any more than our opinions in physics or geometry"; "the opinions of man are not the object of civil government, nor under its jurisdiction"; "truth is great and will prevail if left to herself; that she is the proper and sufficient antagonist to error."[46]

A coalition led by Madison secured the passage of Jefferson's bill in January 1786. The majority of votes came from the evangelical camp, which agreed with the two statesmen on the necessity of preventing the state from subsidizing religion financially but which expected that the churches, once liberated from the state and unleashed, would rout deism. The very deism that Jefferson thought was the only faith fit for a reasonable man would be "put to open shame and its dread Consequences removed."[47] The yawning disparity between Jefferson's attitude toward religion and that of the religious freedom bill's supporters—not to mention the majority of the American people—has prompted historians to call the passage of the bill in 1786 an "anomaly" and to describe Madison and Jefferson's position on religion at that time as "eccentric."[48] This fact has not stopped legal scholars and jurists from putting a Jeffersonian spin on the Virginia assessment controversy—viewing its results as the harbinger of secularism in the public sphere—and using it as a guide to the meaning of the establishment clause of the First Amendment, apparently on the sole grounds that Madison was involved on both occasions.[49] This interpretative strategy is itself eccentric, especially since Jefferson changed his views about religion and its relationship to public life during the 1790s and, during his presidency, offered powerful, heretofore overlooked, symbolic support for the cause of religion.

SIX ⚬

RELIGION AND THE FEDERAL GOVERNMENT

Neither the revolutionary state governments nor the Articles of Confederation gave Americans stability and prosperity. Consequently, a group of energetic, young leaders, responding to a demand (that they themselves had helped stimulate) for a new national government, convened in Philadelphia in May 1787 and in four months produced the federal Constitution, the *summa* of American statecraft. Some Americans have believed that the Constitution was divinely inspired, a fact that the Framers, to the surprise and dismay of numbers of their contemporaries, refused to acknowledge.

"Many pious people," Benjamin Rush complained to John Adams in 1789, "wish the name of the Supreme Being had been introduced somewhere in the new Constitution."[1] A few years later Timothy Dwight returned to the subject: "we found the Constitution without any acknowledgement of God; without any recognition of his mercies to us . . . or even of his existence. The Convention, by which it was formed, never asked, even once, his direction

or his blessing upon their labours."[2] That the Constitution glanced in God's direction—certifying in Article 7 that it was adopted "in the Year of our Lord" 1787 and recognizing, in Article 1, Section 7, the sanctity of the Sabbath by excluding it from the ten days in which a president was obliged to return a bill to Congress—did not appease pious Americans who considered these furtive references proof enough that the Framers had unaccountably turned their backs on the Almighty.

On the surface, at least, it seems that the critics were correct, for there appears to have been a greater poverty of spirit in the Constitutional Convention than in any major official gathering since the first meeting of the Continental Congress in September 1774. Why was this so? Why had men, who, as members of Congress, implored God to intervene on America's behalf or who, as members of state legislatures, pressed for general religious taxes, a short time later forgot God in Philadelphia? The "father of the Constitution," James Madison, is part of the puzzle, for Madison was a mem-

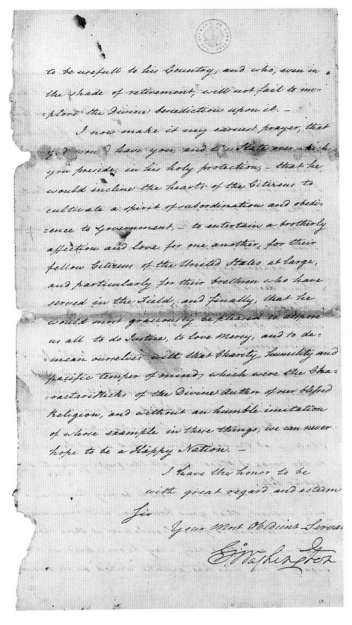

George Washington, circular to the chief executives of the states, June 11, 1783 (last page).
Papers of George Washington, Manuscript Division (LCMS-44693-176).

The draft of the circular letter is in the hand of a secretary, although the signature is Washington's. Some have called this concluding paragraph "Washington's Prayer."

ber of the congressional committee that wrote the fast day proclamation of 1781, begging "our blessed Saviour [for] pardon and forgiveness" and praying that "pure and undefiled religion may universally prevail,"³ and yet, at the Constitutional Convention, he seems to have been oblivious to the divine assistance that a short time before had seemed so essential. To explain the Philadelphia Convention, one would almost think that some sudden, mass apostasy had occurred in America's political elite.

In a famous speech to the Convention on June 28, knowledge of which was suppressed for a time by that body's secrecy rules, Benjamin Franklin offered a clue about the fortunes of religion at Philadelphia. Franklin reproved his fellow delegates for forgetting God, that "powerful Friend" who guided America to victory over the mighty British Empire. I have lived "a long time," Franklin explained, "and the longer I live, the more convincing proofs I see of this Truth—<u>that God governs in the Affairs of Men</u> . . . We have been assured, Sir, in the Sacred Writings, that 'except the Lord build the House, they labour in vain that build it.' I firmly believe this; and I also believe, that, without his concurring Aid, we shall succeed in this political Building no better than the Builders of Babel." Accordingly, Franklin moved that "Prayers, imploring the Assistance of Heaven, and its Blessing on our Deliberations, be held in this Assembly every morning."⁴ After some discussion the motion failed, ostensibly because the Convention had no funds to pay local clergymen to act as chaplains.

The delegates, Franklin scolded, needed to remember what they had done at the First Continental Congress: "in the beginning of the Contest with G. Britain, when we were sensible of danger we had daily prayers in this room for divine protection." What Franklin meant was that in 1774 war was imminent—just after the First Congress convened, reports swept Philadelphia that the British navy had bombarded Boston—and from that moment until at least 1781 every member of Congress—every state and local official, for that matter—was in personal peril. A sudden shift in the war could bring everyone to the gallows as traitors. Consequently, the First and subsequent Congresses were composed of anxious and penitent men who filled its halls and packed its pronouncements with religious language.

Members of the Convention considered that they too were meeting in a time of national crisis, but many of their fellow citizens disagreed, accusing them of exaggerating the nation's problems so that they could personally profit in a new political order of their own devising. Conceding that there was a genuine crisis in 1787, it was a different kind of predicament from the one the nation faced in 1774. No one's life was in danger in 1787. All that could have been hurt by attending the Convention was the participants' egos had they failed to devise a workable new plan of government. In the peaceful, comfortable City of Brotherly Love it may simply not have struck the delegates, as they regaled each other with analyses of ancient and modern republics, that they were in immediate need of divine assistance and protection.

Experience in Congress shaped the delegates' approach to religion in another way as well. Congress launched its religious initiatives with a keen appreciation of the risks involved, for the diversity of the nation's denominations and their passionate attachment to their own confessional procedures always raised the possibility that the most innocent-looking religious measure might offend a powerful segment of the population and shatter the unity necessary to prosecute the war against the British successfully. In 1774, for example, influential members of Congress argued against appointing a chaplain on the grounds that "we were so divided in religious sentiment . . . that we could not join in the same act of worship."[5] Disputes in the states over the various general assessment acts had further sensitized the country's politicians to the divisive potential of religious issues, with the result that in 1787 Convention members hardly needed to be admonished, as John Adams later warned, that "nothing is more dreaded than the national government meddling with religion."[6]

The Convention knew that its proposals to strengthen the national government would be controversial enough, without adding religious reforms to the mix. It wanted the Constitution to be what present-day legislators call a "clean bill," a measure stripped of as many provocative provisions as possible to make it as broadly palatable as possible. The only religious provision written into the new Constitution, the proscription, in Article 6, of religious tests as a qualification for federal officeholders, was intended to promote this objective by satisfying everyone in the body politic, even Jews and Muslims, as observers noted, that they could not be discriminated against—could not suffer civil disabilities because of their religion—under the new regime.

That religion was not otherwise addressed in the Constitution did not make it an "irreligious" document any more than the Articles of Confederation was an "irreligious" document. The Constitution dealt with the church precisely as the Articles had, thereby maintaining, at the national level, the religious status quo. Both documents were understood to be charters of limited powers granted by the people to their representatives (the Constitution, of course, increased the powers granted). In neither document did the people yield any explicit power to act in the field of religion. But the absence of expressed powers did not, as we have seen, prevent the old Congress from sponsoring a broad program to support general, nonsectarian religion nor, as we will presently see, did it stop the Congress under the Constitution, led by men who had served their apprenticeship in the earlier body, from imitating that program. It appears that the nation's legislators, before and after 1787, assumed that they had a limited ability to act as nursing fathers of the church, that neither the Articles of Confederation nor the Constitution denied them a modicum of undefined power to promote religion in the public interest.

When the American people received the new Constitution, many saw nothing in it to prevent ambitious politicians from making experiments on the nation's civil and religious liberties. Thomas Jefferson, George Mason, and other respected statesmen urged that a bill of rights be added to the Constitution to thwart such encroachments. During the ratification debates in the several states, demands for such a measure became too insistent to be ignored. To secure approval of the Constitution, its supporters promised to try to enact a bill of rights as soon as the new government organized itself. To guide its representatives, James Madison among them, in these deliberations, the Virginia Ratifying Convention in July 1788 proposed a series of constitutional amendments, one of which stipulated that "no particular religious sect or society ought to be favored or established by Law in preference to others."[7] Before leaving for the first meeting of the new federal Congress, Madison also heard from the powerful Baptist interest in his district. Reminding him of the "mobs, fines, bonds and prisons" that they had suffered from the Anglican-dominated "regal government," the Baptists entreated Madison to guarantee that the new government would not "favour one system more than another [and] oblige all others to pay to the support of their system as much as they please."[8]

To prevent religious favoritism by the federal government, Madison, in the Bill of Rights that he introduced in Congress on June 8, 1789, directed that no "national religion be established."[9] The adjective "national" was dropped during congressional deliberations on the Bill of Rights and the text of the First Amendment as adopted read: "Congress shall make no law respecting an establishment of religion." For Madison, however, religion in this phrase always retained the original, June 8 meaning of a national religion, as his "Detached Memoranda" indicated. This unpublished, political reminiscence, composed after Madison's second term as president, clarified the specific sense in which he understood the establishment clause. In it, Madison first wrote, "the constitution of the U.S. forbids everything like an establishment of religion," and then corrected himself by adding, with a caret, "a national" in front of religion.[10] To Madison and his colleagues the establishment clause of the First Amendment meant that Congress could not pick out one denomination and promote it to the status of an official national religion by favoring it—and it alone—with tax support and coercive authority. Madison certainly did not believe that this understanding of the establishment clause opened the door for something like a general assessment scheme on the national level, because here the text of the Constitution governed, and it granted Congress no power to legislate on religious matters. But Madison evidently thought that the Constitution conferred some modest degree of authority that would permit the national government to support Christianity in a non-discriminatory, non-coercive way, for he, like his friend Jefferson, did precisely this during his presidency.

The first federal Congress, which convened in

In his Farewell Address, published on September 19, 1796, in the Philadelphia American Daily Advertiser *and immediately reprinted as a pamphlet throughout the United States, Washington advised the American people that he would not seek a third term and offered advice on the country's future policies. The Address was drafted by Alexander Hamilton and revised for publication by Washington himself. Hamilton's draft in the Library's Manuscript Division shows that Washington made only a few significant changes in the religion section of the Address.*

(14)

overbalance in permanent evil any partial or tranfient benefit which the ufe can at any time yield.

Of all the difpofitions and habits which lead to political profperity, religion and morality are indifpenfable fupports. In vain would that man claim the tribute of patriotifm, who fhould labour to fubvert thefe great pillars of human happinefs, thefe firmeft props of the duties of men and citizens. The mere politician, equally with the pious man, ought to refpect and cherifh them. A volume could not trace all their connections with private and public felicity. Let it fimply be afked, where is the fecurity for property, for reputation, for life, if the fenfe of religious obligation *defert* the oaths, which are the inftruments of inveftigation in Courts of Juftice ? And let us with caution indulge the fuppofition, that morality can be maintained without religion. Whatever may be conceded to the influence of refined education on minds of peculiar ftructure ; reafon and experience both forbid us to expect that national morality can prevail in exclufion of religious principle.

'Tis fubftantially true, that virtue or morality is a neceffary fpring of popular government. The rule indeed extends with more or lefs force to every fpecies of free government. Who that is a fincere friend to it can look with indifference upon attempts to fhake the foundation of the fabrick ?

Promote, then, as an object of primary importance, inftitutions for the general diffufion of knowledge. In proportion as the ftructure of a government gives force to public opinion, it is effential that public opinion fhould be enlightened.

As a very important fource of ftrength and fecurity cherifh public credit. One method of preferving it is to ufe it as fparingly as poffible ; avoiding occafions of expence by cultivating peace ; but remembering alfo that timely difburfements to prepare for danger, frequently prevent much greater difburfements to repeal it ; avoiding likewife the accumulation of

April 1789, patterned its religious policies after those of the old Congress. The members attended a church service en masse immediately after Washington was sworn in on April 30, 1789. Officiating at the service was Samuel Provoost (1742–1815), Episcopal bishop of New York, who was appointed congressional chaplain on May 1, along with the Reverend William Linn, a Dutch Reformed pastor. Selecting two chaplains of different denominations, as required by a joint congressional resolution of April 15, copied the policy the old Congress adopted after the defection of Duché in September 1777 and satisfied the revolutionary imperative of treating Christian denominations in an equal, non-preferential fashion. Congress passed legislation, implementing the Confederation Congress's Northwest Ordinance, with its affirmation that "Religion, Morality and knowledge [were] necessary to good government and the happiness of Mankind,"[11] and it also repassed its predecessor's legislation for imposing Christian morality on the army and navy.

On September 25, 1789, the day after the House of Representatives approved the Bill of Rights in its final form, the pious Elias Boudinot, president of Congress, 1782–83, announced to his colleagues that he could not "think of letting the session pass over without offering an opportunity to all the citizens of the United States of joining, with one voice, in returning to Almighty God their sincere thanks for the many blessings that He poured down upon them." Boudinot, therefore, moved that the House and Senate request the President to "recommend to the people of the United States a day of public thanksgiving and prayer, to be observed by acknowledging, with grateful hearts, the many signal favors of Almighty God."[12]

Only two congressmen went on record as opposing Boudinot's motion, Aedanus Burke of South Carolina (1743–1802) and his colleague Thomas Tucker (1745–1828), who took the "strict separationist" position that proclaiming a national day of thanksgiving "is a business with which Congress have nothing to do; it is a religious matter, and, as such, is proscribed to us."[13] Tucker was answered by Roger Sherman (1721–1793), who observed that the "practice of thanksgiving [was] warranted by a number of precedents in Holy Writ," which he mentioned, and were an "example . . . worthy of Christian imitation on the present occasion."[14] Boudinot concluded by citing "further precedents from the practice of the late Congress" which, of course, had approved a whole series of thanksgiving and fast day proclamations. Boudinot's motion passed both houses of Congress with only two recorded objections, and on October 3, 1789, George Washington issued a proclamation recommending that the American people, on November 26, thank God for his "signal and manifold mercies, and the favorable interpositions of his providence" as well as to beseech Him "to pardon our national and other transgressions."[15]

Washington had no reservations about publicly acknowledging the importance of religious faith for the nation's destiny, just as he was always prepared to insist that American citizens enjoy the fullest measure of religious liberty and that American institutions give "to bigotry no sanction."[16] As commander of the Continental Army, Washington frequently invoked God's assistance for the American cause, often in words that made a deep impression on his fellow citizens. They especially cherished his circular to the chief executives of the thirteen states, June 8, 1783, announcing his intention to resign his command and praying that God would "most graciously be pleased to dispose us all, to do Justice, to love mercy, and to demean ourselves with that Charity, humility and pacific temper of mind, which were the Characteristicks of the Divine Author of our blessed Religion, and without an humble imitation of whose example in these things, we can never hope to be a happy Nation."[17]

Washington's most famous valedictory was, of course, his Farewell Address, delivered to the American people on September 19, 1796. Drafted by Alexander Hamilton, the Farewell Address was edited into final form by Washington himself. The section on religion read:

> Of all the dispositions and habits which lead to political prosperity, Religion and morality are indispensable supports. In vain would that man claim the tribute of Patriotism, who should labour to subvert these great Pillars of human happiness, these firmest props of the duties of Men and citizens. The mere Politician, equally with the pious man ought to respect and to cherish them. A volume could not trace all their connections with private and public felicity. Let it simply be asked where is the security for property, for reputation, for life, if the sense of religious obligation <u>deserts</u> the oaths, which are the instruments of investigation in Courts of Justice? And let us with caution indulge the supposition, that morality can be maintained without religion. Whatever may be conceded to the influence of refined education on minds of peculiar structure, reason and experience both forbid us to expect that National

morality can prevail in exclusion of religious principle. 'Tis substantially true, that virtue or morality is a necessary spring of popular government. The rule indeed extends with more or less force to every species of free Government.[18]

In the last sentences, we see once again what might be called the founding generation's syllogism, which occurs repeatedly in every form of discourse from 1776 onward; virtue and morality are necessary for free, republican government; religion is necessary for virtue and morality; religion is, therefore, necessary for republican government.

Washington's successor, John Adams, who unapologetically called himself a "church going animal,"[19] continued his predecessor's policy of offering strong rhetorical support for religion. "Statesmen," Adams contended, "may plan and speculate for Liberty, but it is Religion and Morality alone, which can establish the principles upon which Freedom can securely stand."[20] In his inaugural address, Adams used a well-known phrase from the Declaration of Independence to inform his countrymen that "a decent respect for Christianity [was] among the best recommendations for public service."[21]

In a fast day proclamation, issued on March 23,

***The Providential Detection.* Etching by an anonymous artist, 1800. The Library Company of Philadelphia.**

This cartoon attacking Thomas Jefferson as an infidel develops the theme, used by the Federalists during the presidential campaign of 1800, that Jefferson's intoxication with the religious and political extremism of the French Revolution disqualified him from public office. The eye of God has instigated the American eagle to snatch from Jefferson's hand the "Constitution & Independence" of the United States before he can cast it on an "Altar to Gallic Despotism," whose flames are being fed by the writings of Thomas Paine, Helvetius, Rousseau, and other freethinkers. The paper, "To Mazzei," dropping from Jefferson's right hand, was a 1796 letter that was interpreted by Jefferson's enemies as an indictment of the character of George Washington.

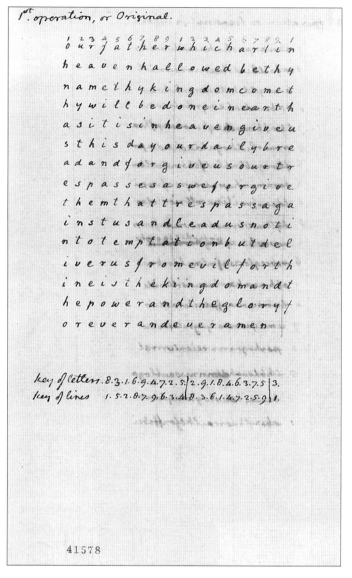

The Lord's Prayer, in Thomas Jefferson's hand. Jefferson Papers, Manuscript Division (LCMS-27748-276).

Jefferson liked to experiment with and use cryptography; there are several different codes in his papers at the Library of Congress. Here is one based on the Lord's prayer, which he carefully wrote out as a block of consecutive letters.

1798, when the nation appeared to be on the brink of a war with France, Adams assumed the posture of a Puritan magistrate addressing a nation that had violated its covenant with God and needed to repent to appease His wrath. "All religious congregations," Adams urged, ought "with the deepest humility, acknowledge before God the manifold sins and transgressions with which we are justly chargeable as individuals and as a nation; beseeching Him at the same time, of His infinite grace, through the Redeemer of the World, freely to remit all our offences, and to incline us, by His Holy Spirit to that sincere repentance and reformation which may afford us reason to hope for his inestimable favor and heavenly benediction."[22] Proclaiming a second national fast the following spring, Adams turned to one of the congressional chaplains, Ashbel Green (1762–1848) for a text. Green's proclamation, issued over Adams' name, was written in what the author called a deliberately "evangelical character";[23] it asserted that there was no truth "more clearly taught in the Volume of Inspiration, nor any more fully demonstrated by the experience of all ages, than that a deep sense and full acknowledgment of the governing providence of a Supreme Being and of the accountableness of men to Him as the searcher of hearts and the righteous distributor of rewards and punishments are conducive equally to the happiness and rectitude of individuals and the well-being of communities."[24]

The election of Thomas Jefferson in 1800 ushered in what scholars have called the "republican revolution," which forever changed the way the country did its business. In religion, Jefferson is pictured as opening the national windows and letting drafts of fresh thinking clear away the musty, moralistic atmosphere created by a quarter century's lecturing by the country's leaders. Under the

Jeffersonian dispensation, the mind was to be set free and reason was to lead the people in new directions. Unconventional ideas would no longer be feared, for, as Jefferson wrote in his *Notes on the State of Virginia*, "it does me no injury for my neighbor to say there are twenty gods, or no god. It neither picks my pocket nor breaks my leg."[25] Those who objected, as did a former congressional chaplain, that "let my neighbor once persuade himself that there is no God and he will soon pick my pocket, and break not only my leg but my neck,"[26] were patronized as being out of touch with the progressive spirit of the age.

The description of Jefferson's presidency as a rebuke to Christianity is a caricature that disregards conflicting evidence that has long been accessible. It has also been undercut by the conclusions of recent scholarship that Jefferson's views on religion underwent changes as he grew older, changes that carried him far from his apparent infatuation with secular moralism in the 1770s and 1780s. Scholars believe that, as a result of reading, sometime around 1793, Joseph Priestley's *An History of the Corruptions of Christianity*, Jefferson experienced a "conversion" to Unitarian Christianity. Priestley's book "amounted almost to a revelation" to Jefferson because it argued—and proved to his satisfaction— that the teachings of Christianity that he found unintelligible and, therefore, unacceptable were additions to and distortions of Christ's original message, foisted off on the faithful over the centuries by self-interested clerics.[27] Christ's real message, according to Priestley, was not much more than a simple, demystified system of morality that was consistent with Jefferson's own conception of what a true religion ought to be. Priestley's book persuaded Jefferson that he was a Christian after all and henceforth he was not reluctant to proclaim the fact to friends.

"I am a Christian," he wrote Benjamin Rush on April 21, 1803, "in the only sense in which he [Jesus] wished any one to be."[28] "I am a real Christian," he wrote Charles Thomson in 1816, "a disciple of the doctrines of Jesus."[29]

When scholars describe Jefferson as being "unusually religious," "sincerely, even profoundly, religious," "the most self-consciously theological of all of America's presidents," they are referring to the post-Priestley phase of his career, the period after the mid-1790s.[30] Beginning in these years and continuing throughout his presidency, Jefferson immersed himself in biblical scholarship, his object being to strain out from the Gospels what he believed to be the genuine sayings of Jesus. The late Eugene Sheridan compared Jefferson's project of "getting back to the plain and unsophisticated precepts of Christ" to Albert Schweitzer's biblical scholarship, describing the president as "the first person in American history to embark upon a quest for the historical Jesus."[31]

The first fruits of Jefferson's efforts to recover the "pure and primitive Gospel" was a forty-six-page compilation, completed at the White House in the spring of 1804, of what he considered to be Jesus's authentic sayings. For Jefferson, biblical exegesis was a snap—"I found the work obvious and easy," he said—the words of Jesus being "as easily distinguishable as diamonds in a dunghill."[32] "The Philosophy of Jesus of Nazareth," as Jefferson called his anthology, has been lost, but after he left the presidency he compiled a more ambitious work, "The Life and Morals of Jesus," usually known as the Jefferson Bible, in which he consulted the New Testament in four languages—Latin, Greek, French, and English—to select what he thought were the best renderings of Jesus's sayings. Jefferson's Bible was a gathering of moral precepts, pruned of the mysterious and miraculous. Such was his passion for privacy that he never shared his version of the scriptures with anyone; its sole purpose was to help him work his way toward a better understanding of the real Christ.[33]

Jefferson's "conversion" to a minimalist Christianity changed his opinion of the value of the faith in civil affairs. He was now prepared to concede what his fellow Founders had been arguing for decades—religion fostered morality and, consequently, had a role to play in a free society. "The Christian religion," he wrote in 1801, when "brought to the original purity and simplicity of its benevolent institutor, is a religion of all others most friendly to liberty."[34] A few years later he informed a Presbyterian minister that "Reading, reflection and time have convinced me that the interests of society require the observation of those moral precepts . . . in which all religions agree."[35] Later still, he indicated that he now agreed with his former opponents that "a future state of retribution for the evil as well as the good done while here" was a crucial concept for the promotion of public morality.[36]

As president, Jefferson put his rejuvenated faith into practice in the most conspicuous form of public witness possible, regularly attending worship services where the delegates of the entire nation could see him—in the "hall" of the House of Representatives. According to recollections of an early Washington insider, "Jefferson during his whole administration, was a most regular attendant. The seat he chose the first day sabbath, and the adjoining one, which his private secretary occupied, were ever afterwords by the courtesy of the congregation, left for him."[37] Contemporary sources confirm that the president "constantly attended public worship in the Hall," once riding through a cloudburst to get to services on time.[38] There are numerous anecdotes about Jefferson's impact on his fellow worshipers,

including one in 1806 about the wife of a New York senator, Catharine Mitchill, stepping on the president's foot at the end of a House service and being "so prodigiously frighten'd that I could not stop to make an apology."[39]

Church services in the House began as soon as the government moved to Washington, in the fall of 1800, as a letter of the Senate chaplain, Thomas Claggett (1783–1816), the Episcopal Bishop of Maryland, reveals: writing to a fellow clergyman on February 18, 1801, Bishop Claggett described "a course of Sermons which I have delivered on Sundays in the Capitol on the truth of the Divine System."[40] From the beginning, services were open to the public and, for a time, they were so popular that the House on Sunday mornings became the rendezvous for the "youth, beauty and fashion" of Washington.[41]

Apparently the House was used because of the shortage of places of worship in the raw, young District of Columbia. Services in the Capitol continued, however, into the 1850s, long after Washington teemed with churches. After the Civil War, from 1865–1868, the House permitted the newly organized First Congregational Church of Washington to use its chambers for church and Sunday school services,[42] at precisely the time, May 13, 1866, when Congress passed the Fourteenth Amendment, which, according to some later judicial theories, forbids religious activities on public property.

There are numerous descriptions of early congressional church services. A Washington newspaper, *The National Intelligencer*, mentioned, for example, an appearance in the House on July 4, 1801, of the Reverend David Austin (1759–1831), who at the time considered himself "struck in prophesy under the style of the 'Joshua' of the American Temple."[43] Having proclaimed to his congressional audience the imminence of the Second Coming of

Christ, Austin took up a collection on the floor of the House to support services he was conducting at "Lady Washington's Chapel" in a nearby hotel, where he was teaching that the "seed of the Millennial estate is found in the backbone of the American Revolution."[44] Nine days earlier, Jefferson contributed, as he noted in his account book, twenty-five dollars "towards fitting up a chapel for Mr. Austin."[45]

Money for religious projects was often raised at services in Congress. A Massachusetts representative, Abijah Bigelow (1775–1860), reported, for example, in 1813, that "two very Christian discourses"—one on 1st Corinthians—were "preached in the hall introductory to a contribution for the purpose of spreading a knowledge of the gospel in Asia."[46]

Ministers of all denominations preached in the House. A British diplomat, Sir Augustus Foster, reported that during Jefferson's administration, "a Presbyterian, sometimes a Methodist, a member of the Church of England, or a Quaker, sometimes even a woman took the Speaker's chair," which was used as the pulpit.[47] From other sources we know that Baptists and Swedenborgians preached in the House. Pious Washingtonians were scandalized in 1821, when the House elected a Unitarian chaplain, Jared Sparks (1789–1866), and invited him to preach on December 23, 1821. An irate Episcopal priest accused the members of having "expelled Jesus Christ from the House" and urged his parishioners to boycott the Capitol until Sparks left.[48] Five years later, the first Roman Catholic House preacher, Bishop John England of Charleston, South Carolina (1786–1842), was accepted with more equanimity. So well received was the bishop's message that it was later published under the title *The Substance of a Discourse Preached in the Hall of the House of Representatives, Jan. 8, 1826* (Baltimore, 1826).

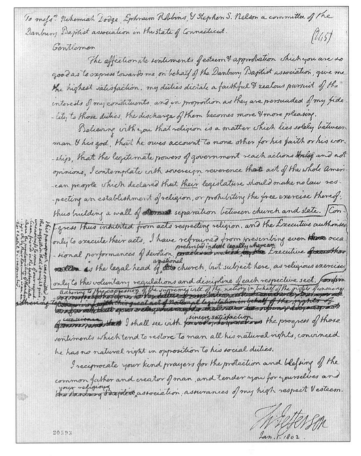

Thomas Jefferson, *To Messrs. Nehemiah Dodge, Ephraim Robbins, & Stephen S. Nelson a committee of the Danbury Baptist Association in the state of Connecticut,* January 1, 1802. Jefferson Papers, Manuscript Division (LCMS-27748-36A and B).

Here is the "Danbury Baptist letter," with its celebrated phrase "a wall of separation between church and state"—note that Jefferson first wrote "a wall of eternal separation"—which American courts have used to interpret the Founders' intentions regarding the relationship between government and religion. The "wall of separation" phrase appears just above the section of the letter that Jefferson circled for deletion. In the deleted section Jefferson explained why he refused to proclaim national days of fasting and thanksgiving, as his predecessors, Adams and Washington, had done. In the left margin, next to the deleted section, Jefferson noted that he excised the section to avoid offending "our republican friends in the eastern states," who cherished days of fasting and thanksgiving.

The nondiscriminatory manner in which the nation's various Christian denominations were permitted to conduct congressional church services seems to have shielded them from controversy and made them politically safe for Jefferson to attend. Notes taken by various congressmen about the texts preachers explicated and about the substance of their sermons make it clear that, during Jefferson's administration, the president and his fellow worshipers received a steady diet of high octane, New Testament Christianity. Consider, for example, the sermon delivered on January 12, 1806, to Jefferson, Vice President Aaron Burr (1756–1836), and a "crowded audience" in the House. The preacher, sizing up the congregation and concluding that "very few" had been born again, broke into an urgent, camp meeting-style exhortation, insisting that "Christ's Body was the Bread of Life and His Blood the drink of the righteous."[49] Although the message was not unusual, the messenger was, for the preacher was a woman, Dorothy Ripley (1767–1832), the first female to conduct religious services in the House (and probably the first woman to speak officially in Congress under any circumstances). An Englishwoman whose father had been "one of Wesley's preachers," Ripley was said to have crossed the Atlantic nineteen times to preach to American audiences.[50] Responding to a vision, received in Whitby, Yorkshire, that she was destined to deliver the Word in the Capitol, Ripley stopped in Washington in December 1805 on an evangelical tour of the southern states and persuaded intermediaries to approach the Speaker of the House, Nathaniel Macon of North Carolina (1757–1837), a Baptist who was "a constant and close reader of the Bible," for permission to preach in the Capitol.[51] When she was informed that Macon had granted her request, Ripley beseeched "the Lord [to] direct my tongue,

Harriet Livermore. **Engraving by J.B. Longacre, from a painting by Waldo and Jewett, 1827. National Portrait Gallery, Smithsonian Institution.**

This image of Harriet Livermore (1788–1868) depicts her in 1827 when she became the second woman to preach in the House of Representatives. Daughter and granddaughter of congressmen, Livermore called herself "the pilgrim stranger," perhaps to convey a sense of the estrangement from male-dominated church hierarchies experienced by her and the other female evangelists—there were at least one hundred—who preached in the United States before the Civil War.

and open my mouth powerfully, that His Name (by a woman) may be extolled to the great astonishment of the hearers, who no doubt will be watching every word to criticize thereon."

Twenty-one years passed before the next woman preached in the House. This time the speaker was better connected than Ripley—her father and grandfather had been members of Congress—and, therefore, in January 1827, she obtained permission to appear in the Capitol with lit-

little difficulty. Ripley's successor was the self-styled "pilgrim stranger," the "conscientiously solitary" evangelical minister, Harriet Livermore (1788–1868).[52] Livermore drew a packed house, including President John Quincy Adams (1767–1848), who "sat on the steps leading up to her feet because he could not find a free chair." Many in the audience wept during her sermon, which, according to a woman who attended, "savored more of inspiration than anything I ever witnessed." Livermore, "who was only one of at least one hundred evangelical women who preached in early national and antebellum America," made additional appearances in Congress in 1832, 1838, and 1843, during which time members of the House also received an impromptu sermon, delivered in the "most sepulchral tones," by "a Quakeress in the Ladies gallery."[53]

Many House preachers during Jefferson's administration took an apologetic approach. On February 27, 1803, for example, a preacher used as his text, "Perfecting holiness in the fear of the Lord." "His plan," according to a congressman who heard him, was "to show the excellence of religion and the importance of a truly religious character."[54] On another occasion, a preacher gave "a very good discourse upon the evidences of the truth of Christianity, and the importance of the Christian religion."[55] On February 5, 1804, Jefferson was present when an Episcopal clergyman, the Reverend Walter Addison (1769–1848), urged public officials to "become models for piety and morality" and then reproached them for "the prophane and blasphemous publications which had been so industriously circulated through our country" which were a "deadly

Manasseh Cutler, diary, January 3, 1802, McCormick Library of Special Collections, Northwestern University Library, Evanston, Illinois.

Manasseh Cutler (1742–1823), a Federalist congressman from Massachusetts, notes in his diary, January 3, 1802, Jefferson's first appearance, as president, at a church service in the House of Representatives, where he attended "constantly" during the remainder of his presidency.

The Old House of Representatives. **Oil on canvas by Samuel F. B. Morse, 1822.**
In the Collection of The Corcoran Gallery of Art, Washington, D.C., Museum Purchase, Gallery Fund.

Church services were conducted in this space, now called Statuary Hall, from 1807 to 1857, when the House moved to its present space. The first services in the Capitol, held when the government moved to Washington in the fall of 1800, were conducted in the "hall" of the House in the north wing of the building. In 1801 the House moved to temporary quarters in the south wing, called the "Oven," which it vacated in 1804, returning to the north wing for three years. Services were conducted in the House until after the Civil War.

poison . . . to the young [and] the uninformed."[56] That December the House received another dose of millennial preaching, this time from the Baltimore Swedenborgian, the Reverend John Hargrove (1750–1839), who spoke on "the Second Coming of Christ, and on the Last Judgment."[57]

Some House preachers assumed a prophetic posture, the most notable seer being the Reverend James Brackinridge (1766–1841), pastor of Washington's First Presbyterian Church, who was known for his innovative exegesis, an example being his sermon in the House on May 29, 1812, in which "he asserted that the Cloths of the Jews on their leaving Egypt lasted 40 Years."[58] Shortly thereafter, "in the plainest and boldest language of reprehension," Brackinridge assailed the members of both houses of Congress for desecrating the Sabbath, warning that "it is the government that will be punished" for the sins of its members; "as with Nineveh of old, it will not be the habitations of the people, but your temples and your palaces that will be burned to the ground." After the British torched the Capitol in 1814, Dolley Madison (1768–1849), who had heard Brackinridge's "threatening sermon" in the House, presumably in the company of her husband,

Members of the United States Marine Corps Band, c. 1798 (detail).
Original art by Lt. Col. Donna Neary, USMC.
Courtesy of "The President's Own"
United States Marine Band, Washington, D.C.

According to Margaret Bayard Smith, a regular at early church services in the Capitol, the Marine Band "made quite a dazzling appearance in the gallery. The marches they played were good and inspiring, but in their attempts to accompany the psalm-singing of the congregation, they completely failed and after a while, the practice was discontinued."

told the preacher that she had "little thought [that his] denunciation would so soon be realized."[59]

How did attending church services in Congress, which was, after all, public property, square with the constitutional scruples generally imputed to Jefferson about mixing the religious and public spheres? Perhaps he reasoned that, since the House of Representatives, a member of a separate and independent branch of the government, was organizing and sponsoring the services, his principles would not be unduly compromised. This would not explain, however, why Jefferson permitted executive branch employees under his direct control, members of the Marine Band, to participate in House church services. Splendidly attired in their scarlet uniforms, the Marine musicians made a "dazzling appearance" in the House on Sundays, as they tried to help the congregation by providing instrumental accompaniment to its psalm singing.[60]

The assistance of the Marine Band was a modest contribution to religion in the capital compared to Jefferson's decision to let executive branch buildings, the War Office and the Treasury, be used for church services. Episcopal services in the War Office were announced in the *National Intelligencer* on May 15, 1801, and Jefferson seems to have approved the use of the Treasury shortly thereafter, for, on July 1, 1801, the *Museum* reported a Baptist service in the building, led by a Mr. Richards of Baltimore. Both buildings were available to all denominations, but Episcopalians and Presbyterians seem to have used them most frequently. A Presbyterian congregation led by the Reverend James Laurie (1778–1853), who is said to have offended Jefferson by a sermon he preached in the Capitol on 2nd Peter: 2, settled into the Treasury building.[61] Four Treasury officials were influential members of Laurie's church; the ruling elder of the church, Joseph Nourse, was the Register of the Treasury. He gave Laurie a sinecure

Manasseh Cutler, diary, December 23, 1804.
McCormick Library of Special Collections,
Northwestern University Library, Evanston, Illinois.

Cutler here describes the Reverend James Laurie officiating over a four-hour communion service in the Treasury Building.

John Quincy Adams, diary, February 2, 1806,
Adams Family Papers, Massachusetts Historical Society,
Boston, Massachusetts.

Adams here describes the Reverend James Laurie, pastor of the Presbyterian Church that had settled into the Treasury Building, preaching to an overflow audience in the Supreme Court chamber.

Catharine Akerly Mitchill, letter to her sister
Margaret Miller, April 8, 1806,
Catharine Mitchill Papers,
Manuscript Division (LCMS-34819-3).

Catharine Mitchill describes to her sister Margaret how she accidently stepped on Jefferson's toes at a church service in the House of Representatives in April 1806.

Charles B. Boynton, fund-raising brochure, Washington, November 1, 1867. Broadside Collection, Rare Book and Special Collections Division.

Charles Boynton (1806–1883) was, in 1867, chaplain of the House and organizing pastor of the First Congregational Church in Washington, which was trying at that time to raise funds to build its own sanctuary. In the meantime, the church, as Boynton informed potential donors, was holding services "at the Hall of Representatives" where "the audience is the largest in town." In fact, "nearly 2000 assembled every Sabbath" for services, making the congregation in the House "the largest Protestant Sabbath audience then in the United States." The First Congregational Church met in the House from 1865 to 1868.

appointment as clerk in his office to supply him with the financial wherewithal to conduct his ministry. Church services in the executive branch buildings were more "religious" than those in the Capitol, because the sacraments were celebrated in the former but not, apparently, in the latter.

Massachusetts Representative Manasseh Cutler (himself a minister of the Gospel) described a communion service (December 23, 1804), conducted by the Reverend Laurie in the Treasury building: "Attended worship at the Treasury. Mr. Laurie alone. Sacrament. Full assembly. Three tables; service very solemn; nearly four hours."[62] John Quincy Adams recorded in his diary another four-hour Presbyterian communion service, conducted by two ministers, in the War Office on January 29, 1804.

During Jefferson's administration, church services were also conducted in the Supreme Court's chambers—both Cutler and Adams describe them[63]—which is not surprising, since Chief Justice John Marshall, who must have approved the services in the Court, had voted for a general religious tax as a member of the Virginia Assembly in 1784 and later served as vice-president of the American Bible Society.

It is no exaggeration to say that, on Sundays in Washington during Thomas Jefferson's presidency, the state became the church. This fact is so contrary to received opinion about Jefferson's religious policies, which picture him as championing the divorce of state from church, that some explanation is required. Jefferson's principal pronouncement, as president, on the relation between government and religion was his famous letter of January 1, 1802, to the Danbury Baptist Association in which he asserted that there should be a "wall of separation between Church and State."[64] The "wall of separation" metaphor has become a household phrase in the United States because the Supreme Court has declared it to be a shorthand expression for "the authoritative declaration of the scope and effect" of the religious section of the Bill of Rights, the establishment clause of the First Amendment.[65] The Court has frequently recurred to Jefferson's metaphor, declaring, in 1947, that "The wall must be kept high and impregnable. We could not approve the slightest breach."[66]

There has been an enormous and continuing controversy about what Jefferson meant by the "wall of separation" metaphor. Aware that, in various writings, including his Second Inaugural Address, Jefferson conceded to state governments the power

The Old Supreme Court Chamber, 1810–60, U.S. Capitol Building.
Photograph by Franz Jantzen, Collection of the Supreme Court of the United States.

Descriptions of church services in the Supreme Court chamber by Manasseh Cutler (1804) and John Quincy Adams (1806) show that services were apparently held in the Court from the moment the government moved to Washington in 1800.

to "discipline" religion, scholars have argued that he penned the "wall of separation" phrase from the congenial perspective of federalism, that is that he meant the phrase to apply only to the activities of the federal government and not to all jurisdictions in the land.[67] If so, what were the implications of the wall metaphor for the federal government?

Jefferson's purpose in writing the Danbury Baptist letter was to point out "why I do not proclaim fastings and thanksgivings as my predecessors did."[68] He drafted, then deleted, a passage in the letter which, when read in conjunction with his other statements on the subject,[69] explained why he repudiated a settled practice that had begun a quarter century earlier. For Jefferson, proclaiming national religious observances smacked of a reversion to the old, tyrannical project of imposing *uniform* religious exercises on the population. Jefferson was advised, however, that, by renouncing fasts and thanksgivings, he ran the risk of alienating his pious New England supporters, of giving "uneasiness to some of our republican friends in the eastern States where the proclamation of thanksgivings etc. by their Executive is an ancient habit & is respected."[70] In other words, Jefferson's principled aversion to proclaiming national religious observances, implicit in the final version of his Danbury Baptist letter, carried with it a potential political cost which he tried to counteract by attending church services in Congress.

It is no accident that Jefferson issued the Danbury Baptist letter on Friday, January 1, 1802, and two days later, on Sunday, January 3, "contrary to all former practice," went to his first church service in the House, which he attended "constantly" for the next seven years.[71] The Danbury letter and Jefferson's commencement of attendance at congressional church services fit together like hand and glove. They must be understood as being bracketed together as part of a carefully balanced strategy of words and action to convey his policy on church and state to his fellow citizens. Jefferson was a master of using the symbolic act to communicate public policy. At the beginning of his administration he appeared at public events in casual clothing to signal the triumph of plain democracy over tinseled aristocracy, a gesture that was a huge hit with his fellow countrymen. He knew that knowledge of his attendance at congressional church services would swiftly spread into the remotest parts of the nation and, soon enough, information about his act of public witness reached the Pennsylvania frontier, where his mentor, Priestley, was now living. "He cannot be far from us," wrote Priestley, "he now attends public worship very regularly."[72]

By attending church services in Congress, Jefferson intended to send to the nation the strongest symbol possible that he was a friend of religion, hoping thereby to retain the political support of pious New England republicans who might be misled by the uncompromising sound of the "wall of separation" metaphor in his letter to their Danbury brethren into believing the slanders of his implacable opponents that he was an infidel or worse. On a policy level, Jefferson used the wall of separation metaphor in the sense of a wall of segmentation, as a partition demarcating the religious activities the government could and could not support. In his view, the government could not be a party to any attempt to impose upon the country a uniform religious exercise or observance; it could, on the other hand, support, as being in the public interest, voluntary, non-discriminatory religious activity, including church services, by putting at its disposal public property, public facilities, and public personnel, including the president himself.

The Danbury Initiative—the letter plus the

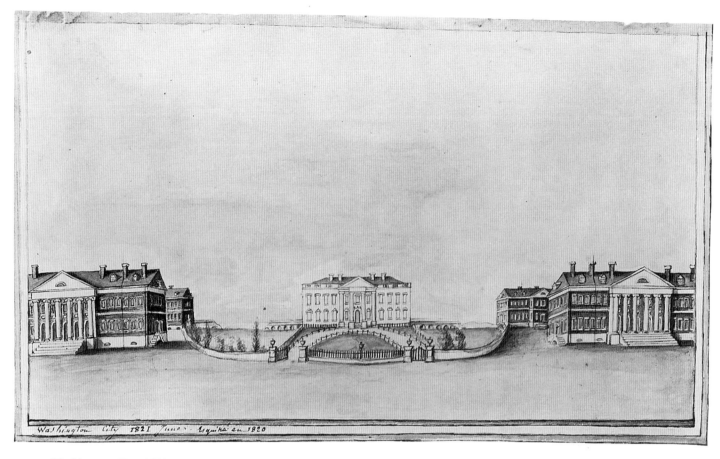

Washington City, 1820. **Photocopy of watercolor sketch by Baroness Hyde de Neuville, 1820, in the collections of the New York Public Library. Prints and Photographs Division (LC-USZ62-44268).**

The first Treasury Building, where several denominations conducted church services, was burned by the British in 1814. The new build-ing, seen here at the lower right, was built on approximately the same location as the earlier one, within view of the White House.

attendance at worship—demonstrates that the ma-ture Jefferson's views on religion and public policy were consistent with those of his fellow Founders, the only difference being the mode of expression, his being symbolic, theirs rhetorical.

Jefferson also underwrote his views with his money, providing financial support during his presi-dency for at least nine local churches (ten, if David Austin's millennial "chapel" is counted). Like other aspects of his religious life, Jefferson's benefactions

have been overlooked by scholars. Stories of his generosity survive in the lore of local congrega-tions, often surfacing in amateurish anniversary his-tories. Most of these traditions prove, upon exami-nation, to be true, for they can be confirmed by consulting Jefferson's account books. From them, we learn that he subscribed considerable sums to the building fund of Christ Church (Washington's first Episcopal congregation),[73] to the building funds of Washington's and Alexandria's First Baptist

Churches,[74] to the Reverend James Chambers' "Independent Protestant Church" of Alexandria (in which Dorothy Ripley preached in 1806 after the city's other pulpits were closed to her),[75] to the Georgetown Methodist Church, and to the building fund of Trinity United Methodist Church in Alexandria, which needed a bigger building to accommodate a flood of members produced by the powerful local revival of 1802–4.[76] In addition, an 1843 copy of the original records (now lost) of St. John's Episcopal Church, Georgetown, shows that in 1803 Jefferson contributed through an intermediary to that congregation's building fund.[77] Surprisingly, in view of Jefferson's well-known aversion to Calvinist dogma, the records of the Georgetown Presbyterian Church show that he contributed $75 to the expansion of its sanctuary. More surprising still, considering the umbrage Jefferson allegedly took at a House sermon preached by James Laurie, was his contribution of $50 for a new church on F Street for Laurie's Presbyterian congregation that had been using the Treasury building.[78]

Another local tradition about Jefferson's religious practices can also be verified by consulting his account books. It is well documented that, when Jefferson first moved to Washington, he attended services at Christ Church, then meeting in a converted tobacco barn on the southeast side of Capitol Hill.[79] The rector of the church, Andrew T. McCormick (1761–1841), was said to be a favorite of his.[80]

Abijah Bigelow, letter to Hannah Bigelow, December 28, 1812.
Courtesy, American Antiquarian Society, Worcester, Massachusetts.

Bigelow, a Federalist congressman from Massachusetts, describes President James Madison at a church service in the House on December 27, 1812, as well as an incident that had occurred when Jefferson was in attendance some years earlier.

McCormick was succeeded in 1823 by the Reverend Ethan Allen, who claimed in a handwritten history, "Washington Parish, Washington City," now in the Manuscript Division of the Library of Congress, that Jefferson "always" sent McCormick "on the morning after new years a note with $50 enclosed in it."[81] That this claim is supported by entries in the president's account book[82] lends plausibility to an anecdote the Reverend Allen recorded in his history. Jefferson, according to Allen, was walking to church one Sunday "with his large red prayer book under his arm when a friend querying him after their mutual good morning said which way are you walking Mr. Jefferson. To which he replied to Church Sir. You going to Church Mr. J. You do not believe a word in it. Sir said Mr. J. No nation has ever yet existed or been governed without religion. Nor can be. The Christian religion is the best religion that has been given to man and I as chief Magistrate of this nation am bound to give it the sanction of my example. Good morning Sir." While this colloquy may not be a literal transcription, it is uncannily close in spirit to Jefferson's attitude and actions as president.

James Madison's actions as president show that his attitude was also within the Founding consensus. On June 7, 1812, Foster, the British minister, reported seeing him leaving church services in the Capitol in a coach and four[83]—Jefferson always came on horseback—and, during the War of 1812, a Navy chaplain preached on Matthew 5:9, "blessed are the peacemakers," while he was in the congregation[84]—thus symbolically signaling his approval for public support of religion. Madison also reverted to the earlier policy of Washington, Adams, and the Continental Congress, proclaiming on four occasions between 1812 and 1815 national days of thanksgiving.

In his Detached Memoranda Madison criticized the religious policies he approved as a member of Congress and followed as president—the appointment of chaplains and the proclamations of days of fasting and thanksgiving—suggesting there may have been some substance to the charges of critics that he was an opportunist, ever willing to sacrifice his constitutional convictions for political popularity. On the other hand, there seems to have been a tension between Madison's religious and constitutional views that may account for the statements in the Detached Memoranda. Although his writings reveal none of the restless religious curiosity of Jefferson, he was considered by the third president to be an expert on matters of faith and practice and, in 1824, was asked by Jefferson to compile a list of theological works for the library of the University of Virginia. Although Madison professed to be "less qualified for the task than you seem to think," he complied with his neighbor's request.[85] That Jefferson did not misjudge his friend's regard for religion is shown by Madison's testimonial in 1825 to the theologian Frederick Beasley (1777–1845): "the belief in a God All Powerful wise & good, is so essential to the moral order of the World & to the happiness of man, that arguments which enforce it cannot be drawn from too many sources nor adopted with too much solicitude to the different characters & capacities to be impressed with it."[86]

Madison approved the results of the revivals that rolled through Virginia during the early years of the nineteenth century. In a letter written in 1819 he seemed to relish the troubles of the Anglican—now Episcopal—church, whose places of worship, "built under the establishment at the public expense, have in many instances gone to ruin, or are in a very dilapidated state, owing chiefly to a desertion of the flocks to other worships." That the defecting evangelical flocks gathered in "Meeting Houses . . . of the plainest and cheapest sort" was, for Madison, a recommendation, not a reproach. He believed that "on a general comparison of the present and former times the balance is clearly and vastly on the side of the present, as to the number of religious teachers, the zeal which actuates them, the purity of their lives, and the attendance of the people on their instructions."[87] Although there is no evidence that Madison was a closet evangelical, it seems apparent that, late in life, he retained substantial sympathy for the doctrine of the new birth and for its social consequences that he had learned long ago at Princeton.

SEVEN ❧

RELIGION AND THE NEW REPUBLIC

The plain, cheap meeting houses that, in the early nineteenth century, dominated the landscape around James Madison's residence in central Virginia were built by Baptists and Methodists, converted during one of the many rounds of revivals that coursed, almost continuously, through the United States from 1800 to the Civil War. During this period, revivalism, through which evangelical religion now found its expression, was "the grand absorbing theme" of American life.[1] Few Americans could escape the evangelical orbit and fewer still wanted to. During some years in the first half of the nineteenth century, revivals occurred so often that religious publications that specialized in tracking them lost count. In 1827, for example, one journal exalted that "revivals, we rejoice to say, are becoming too numerous in our country to admit of being generally mentioned in our Record."[2] The same could be said for many other years between the inaugurations of Jefferson and Lincoln, years in which historians see "evangelicalism emerging as a kind of national church or national religion."[3]

What was the condition of the country's religion in the 1790s on the eve of the great wave of revivals? Predictably, the nation's clergy thought that it was deplorable. Like broken records, they intoned the old dirges about "declension." In May 1798, for example, the General Assembly of the Presbyterian Church beat its collective breast: "we perceive, with pain and fearful apprehension, a general dereliction of religious principle and practice among our fellow citizens . . . the profligacy and corruption of public morals have advanced with a progress proportional to our declension in religion."[4] Young people, as usual, were viewed as barometers of the encroaching barbarism. Just as Jonathan Edwards, in the 1730s, brooded over the teenagers of Northampton, for "nightwalking" and assembling "in conventions of both sexes, for mirth and jollity," so Connecticut ministers, in the 1790s, complained that their youthful charges "spent too much time at balls." It was even reported that some Yale students were keeping wine in their rooms. There was no question, said the Reverend John Ely in 1798, that "in this day of so general declension . . . vice and irreligion abound."[5]

Recent scholarship has provided a rather different picture of American religion during the last decade of the eighteenth century. There were, we now know, revivals from one end of the country to another: one in Georgia in 1787; "an intense but local interdenominational revival" in Virginia from 1787 through 1789; another in Baltimore in 1789, complete with "gushing tears," "writhing agitations," and "convulsive throes of the human body"; one in Boston in 1790; another in central North Carolina in 1791; and a "precious harvest" in Connecticut in 1792.[6] These spiritual showers led an historian to conclude that "after 1790 signs of renewed religious vigor appeared throughout the country."[7] One of the few inquiries into church membership in the 1790s revealed that about 50 percent of the citizens of Baltimore attended services, prompting the author of the study to reject the "myth of the great decline" of religion in the 1790s.[8]

It appears, then, that American clergymen succumbed to the temptation—indulged an occupational disposition?—of exaggerating the decay of religion around them. There was, however, one new and, to the faithful, alarming aspect of the religious scene in the 1790s: the publication by American celebrities of unbridled assaults on Christianity. The hero of Ticonderoga, Ethan Allen, set the example with his *Reason the Only Oracle of Man* (1784), but the most withering broadside was fired by Thomas Paine (1737–1809) in his *Age of Reason* (1794). Paine's book, which was unsettling because of the author's fame and his powers of persuasion, was something new under the sun in America, an out-

right mockery of the fundamental elements of the Christian faith. Paine, for example, scoffed at the virgin birth as "blasphemously obscene." The temptation of Jesus after his baptism was ridiculed. Why, Paine asked, did Satan show the Savior no republics: "is it only with Kingdoms that his sooty highness has any interest?"[9]

For the orthodox, Paine's book symbolized "infidelity" and the malign influence of the atheistic French Revolution, whose adherents, like the Bolsheviks of our own century, were suspected of sponsoring a world-wide campaign to subvert Christianity. Fears of infidelity were fanned by trifles like smart-alecky college students saluting each other as "Citoyen" and reached a panic among certain New Englanders who convinced themselves that a European secret society, the Bavarian Illuminati, had established outposts on American soil with the intention of overthrowing religion and government alike. "Shall our sons become the disciples of Voltaire and the dragoons of Marat," thundered Timothy Dwight in 1798, "or our daughters the concubines of the Illuminati?"[10]

The infiltration of the Illuminati was just as imaginary as fears that "republican religion" on the French revolutionary model would conquer the United States. America in the 1790s remained solidly committed to Christianity; without widespread devotion to the faith it is, in fact, impossible to account for the massive revivals that began around 1800 and that deserve to be called the true "republican religion" of the new nation.

During the presidency of John Adams, major revivals began at the eastern and western edges of the United States and passed each other heading in opposite directions. The Second Great Awakening started in Connecticut in 1797 and quickly spread through New England; by 1802 it had reached

Sacramental Scene in a Western Forest. **Lithograph by P. S. Duval, c. 1801, from Joseph Smith, *Old Redstone* (Philadelphia, 1854). General Collections (LC-USZ62-119893).**

The Kentucky revivals originated with Presbyterians and emerged from marathon outdoor "Communion seasons," which were a feature of Presbyterian practice in Scotland.

northeast Ohio. The western revival began at Gaspar River, Kentucky, in the summer of 1800 and moved east to North Carolina by 1801; by 1803 it had swept through the entire southern seaboard.

Although the Second Great Awakening in New England was led by disciples and descendants of Jonathan Edwards and occurred in the same area as the First Great Awakening, the ferment in distant Kentucky was closer in spirit to the earlier revival in the passions of its preachers, the responses of its audiences, and the controversies it generated. The New England revival was conducted with a sobriety missing sixty years earlier: there were no wild-eyed itinerants, no split congregations, no massive, open-air meetings, and no carnivals of public emotion.

"Outcries, distortions of the body, or any symptoms of intemperate zeal," were absent. "You might," reported an observer, "often see a congregation sit with deep solemnity depicted in their countenances, without ever observing a tear or sob during the service."[11] Since these decorous proceedings were universally approved, they continued in some New England locations for decades. At Yale College, for example, there were fifteen sustained revivals between 1800 and 1840. Connecticut became so saintly that foreign visitors were happy to hurry through "the dullest, most disagreeable state in the union."[12]

Dull, Kentucky was not. The spiritual excitement there reminded observers of the Day of Pentecost. Like the events in New England, the Kentucky revivals had a Great Awakening pedigree, for, in their initial stages, they were led by Presbyterian ministers who had been trained in New Side schools sponsored by Gilbert Tennent and his associates and staffed by disciples and admirers of that redoubtable companion of Whitefield. Pupils of such teachers naturally preached old-fashioned Calvinist doctrines like original sin and its corollary, the "terrors of the law," admonishing audiences that, unless they re-

pented of their sins, they would be consumed by the wrath of a just God. The message that Presbyterian preachers delivered on the frontier to audiences of Scotch-Irish pioneers, bred in a tradition of demonstrative religious revivalism, could have been lifted from a sermon of Gilbert Tennent. Consider, for example, James McGready (c. 1758–1817), a leading western Presbyterian evangelist, of whom it was said that "he would so array hell before the wicked that they tremble and quake, imagining a

Religious Camp Meeting. **Watercolor by J. Maze Burbank, c. 1839.**
Old Dartmouth Historical Society-New Bedford Whaling Museum, New Bedford, Massachusetts.
Gift of William F. Havemeyer.

In 1839 Burbank exhibited at the Royal Society in London this watercolor of "a camp meeting, or religious revival in America, from a sketch taken on the spot." It is not known where or exactly when the revival painted by Burbank occurred.

lake of fire and brimstone yawning to overwhelm them and the hand of the Almighty thrusting them down the horrible abyss."[13]

If the theology of the Kentucky revivals was not new, neither was their ecumenicism. In the West, Presbyterians, Baptists, and Methodists preached to crowds in the open air side by side, but Whitefield, the Anglican, had anticipated these developments by appearing in Presbyterian and Congregational meeting houses and by asserting that conversion was more important than the denomination that delivered it. There was nothing really new, then, in declarations by preachers like McGready that "in that awful day, when the universe assembled, must appear before the quick and the dead, the question brethren, will not be, were you a Presbyterian— Seceder—Covenanter—a Baptist—or a Methodist: but, did you experience a new birth?"[14]

The crowds in Kentucky, though they seemed prodigious to participants, were no bigger than some that Whitefield and Tennent drew. But they looked different. First Great Awakening audiences usually came from towns and cities and convened on short notice. In Kentucky and in other frontier areas, audiences came from great distances by wagon, packed with provisions to sustain families for several days. When assembled, usually in clearings in the wilderness, these conventions of frontier farmers became camp meetings—a unique American contribution to religious history.

The largest and most famous Kentucky camp meeting took place at Cane Ridge in Bourbon County in August 1801. As many as twenty-five thousand people (twelve times the population of Kentucky's largest city) may have met at Cane Ridge for marathon day-night services, conducted by eighteen Presbyterian and several Baptist and Methodist ministers, using stumps and fallen logs

for pulpits. "The noise," recalled a participant, "was like the roar of Niagara. The vast sea of human beings seemed to be agitated as if by a storm."[15] "At night," wrote another eye witness:

the whole scene was awfully sublime. The ranges of tents, the fires, reflecting light amidst the branches of the towering trees; the candles and lamps illuminating the encampment; hundreds moving to and fro, with lights or torches, like Gideon's army; the preaching, praying, singing and shouting, all heard at once, rushing from different parts of the ground, like the sound of many waters, was enough to swallow up all the powers of contemplation. Sinners falling, and shrieks and cries for mercy awakened in the mind a lively apprehension of the scene, when the awful sound will be heard, 'arise ye dead and come to Judgment.'[16]

The excitement at Cane Ridge and other frontier revivals produced physical manifestations that puzzled their Presbyterian promoters. The boisterous animation they encountered struck them as "new and passing strange"; "the falling down of multitudes and their crying out," they repeatedly claimed, "was to us so new a scene that we thought it prudent not to be over hasty" in judging it.[17] The surprise of the Presbyterian preachers is itself surprising, for striking physical expressions had been a common and controversial feature of the First Great Awakening. Had their teachers not told them about Whitefield's appearance at the New Side stronghold at Faggs Manor, Pennsylvania, in 1740, where "bitter cries and groans pierce[d] the hardest heart"? "Some of the people were as pale as death; others were wringing their hands; others lying on the ground; others sinking into the arms of friends; most lifting up their eyes to Heaven and crying for mercy."[18]

Bishops of the A.M.E. Church. **Engraving by John H.W. Burley, Washington, D.C., 1876. Printed by J.H. Daniels, Boston. Prints and Photographs Division (LC-USZ62-15059).**

In the center is Richard Allen, founder of the African Methodist Episcopal Church, surrounded by ten bishops of the church. At the upper left and right corners are pictures of Wilberforce University and Payne Institute; other scenes in the life of the church are depicted, including the sending of missionaries to Haiti in 1824.

Perhaps what surprised the Presbyterian preachers were the innovations and exaggerations that cropped up in Kentucky: the rolling exercise, the "barking" exercise, in which new converts, like coon dogs, "treed" the devil; and the "jerks," during which the heads of participants "would jerk back suddenly, frequently causing them to yelp or make some other involuntary noise . . . sometimes the head would fly every way so quickly that their fea-

tures could not be recognized." Heads often moved back and forth so fast "that the hair of females would be made to crack like a carriage whip," showering bystanders with hair pins.[19]

Conservatives, as Charles Chauncey and his supporters had done in 1743, used the emotional and physical exuberance of the Kentucky revivals to denounce them as frauds. Resurrected was the old canard that the revivals were little more than sex orgies, a charge that Timothy Cutler had made sixty years ago in Boston, when he asserted that "our presses are teeming with books and our women with bastards."[20] Now it was said that, in Kentucky, "more souls were begot than saved."[21]

These assaults had their effect, with the result that Presbyterians and Baptists soon renounced the use of camp meetings. Methodists, however, redoubled their efforts to organize and disciple the meetings and they quickly became their ecclesiastical signature. It was under Methodist auspices that the camp meetings spread from Kentucky eastward into the southern seaboard states in the period after Cane Ridge. By 1802, Methodist meetings, attended by upwards of ten thousand people and scores of preachers, blossomed in Georgia and South Carolina. The next year camp meetings were in full swing in Virginia; one enthusiast reported attending twenty-three in the Old Dominion between March 1804 and April 1805.[22]

The Potomac River was no barrier to the Methodists, who, by the end of the first decade of the nineteenth century, had brought their brand of revivalism to the bustling cities of the Northeast. There was a "remarkable" Methodist revival in New York City in 1808, followed by major revivals in the next decade in Philadelphia, Baltimore, and Providence.[23] In the eastern cities Methodism met the more sedate style of New England revivalism, inching southward from its stronghold in Connecticut. Sober preaching, prayer and fasting, and private pastoral counseling enabled the judicious Reverend Gardiner Spring (1785–1873) to produce a revival in New York's Brick Presbyterian Church in 1815, but men of Spring's training and deportment could not reach the mass of humble city dwellers who flocked to Methodist services that, "impatient of scriptural restraint and moderation," often ex-

ploded into the "clapping of hands, screaming and even jumping."[24] Methodists placed the big cities under siege by staging camp meetings on their outskirts and channeling the enthusiasm generated there into fervent evangelical services in their center city churches. The Methodists introduced into the urban churches soul-saving techniques that had been tried and tested in the frontier camp meetings— prolonged meetings, prayers for individuals by name, participation of women in services, and especially, the "mourner's bench" or "anxious seat," a reserved area in front of the pulpit where those under concern for their souls could be separated from the congregation at large and be ministered to by the pastor and his associates, receiving special attention (psychological coercion, critics charged) intended to speed conversion.

Scholars now credit the Methodists with bringing the "lusty breath of the western revival into the East," an achievement formerly attributed to Charles Grandison Finney (1792–1875), a Presbyterian who captured the nation's attention in the 1820s.[25] Finney's importance should not be underestimated, however, for, after some initial resistance, he made the "new measures," pioneered by the Methodists, palatable to the conservative eastern evangelical establishment and secured its cooperation in his own efforts, beginning in 1830–31, to convert the big cities along the Atlantic Coast. Finney's accomplishments in urban America were welcomed by evangelical advocates in all denominations. It is "no small consolation," wrote a Methodist in 1831, to "see our large Atlantic and commercial cities, which exert so great an influence over the surrounding country, taking the lead in [the] present great revivals of pure religion. In Baltimore, New York, New Haven, and Boston, and other cities, God is doing wonders."[26]

Finney's first successes occurred in that region of western New York state known as the Burned Over District, because of the frequency with which it had been seared by the fires of revivalism. Between 1800 and 1830 the nation itself (east of the Alleghenies) can be thought of as a giant burned over district, for during this period no region was too remote to have been at least singed by evangelical religion. Evangelicalism's hegemony in 1830, established by revivalism, can be read in membership roles of the nation's denominations. Those churches that embraced and sponsored it dwarfed those that spurned it. The Baptists and Methodists were in a virtual dead heat in 1830 as the nation's largest denomination, with the Presbyterians a strong third. The growth rate of all three denominations was remarkable. The Methodists, for example, starting with fewer than 10,000 members in 1780, numbered 250,000 in 1820, doubled to 500,000 by 1830, and doubled again during the next decade to become, by 1844, the nation's largest denomination with 1,068,525 members, 3,988 itinerant preachers, and 7,730 local preachers.[27]

Presbyterians would have registered stronger numbers had the denomination not been rent by several schisms, resulting directly from theological differences over the meaning and consequences of the western revivals. A notable defector was the organizer of the Cane Ridge revival, Barton Stone (1772–1844), who, in 1804, gathered about him a group of followers who called themselves, simply, "Christians" and who joined in 1832 with admirers of Alexander Campbell (1788–1866), another dissenter from orthodox Presbyterianism, to form the Disciples of Christ. Numbers of western Presbyterians split off into what became the Cumberland Presbyterian Church, while a few others joined the United Society of Believers in Christ's Second Appearing, or Shakers, a sect founded in England by "Mother" Ann Lee (1736–1784), who was held by the faithful to be an incarnation of Christ, and who sent emissaries to Kentucky to spy out the land.

Schisms during the floodtide of revivalism also occurred in the ranks of African-American Christianity. Scholars disagree about the extent of the native African content of black Christianity as it emerged in eighteenth-century America,[28] but there is no dispute that the Christianity of the black population was grounded in evangelicalism. The Presbyterian evangelist, Samuel Davies (1723–1761), is credited, during the First Great Awakening in Virginia, with being one of the first ministers to offer religious instruction to slaves. Quakers, following the example of Anthony Benezet (1713–1784) and John Woolman (1720–1772), pressed for the abolition of slavery well before the American Revolution. However, the Friends, being cool to the evangelical style, attracted far fewer members than did the Baptists and Methodists, who reaped large harvests in the black communities, principally because they treated blacks as brothers and sisters in Christ and encouraged gifted black preachers to speak to all audiences.

The Second Great Awakening has been called the "central and defining event in the development of Afro-Christianity."[29] During these revivals Methodists and Baptists converted large numbers of blacks; according to a contemporary estimate, there were, by 1815, forty thousand black Methodists and an equal number of black Baptists.[30] Many blacks were, nevertheless, disappointed at the treatment they received from their fellow believers, especially at the backsliding in the commitment to abolish slavery which fired many white Baptists and Methodists immediately after the American Revolution.[31] Blacks responded by trying to establish as much autonomy as possible within the Baptist and Methodist denominational frameworks. When discontent

Mrs. Juliann Jane Tillman, Preacher of the AME Church.
Engraving by P. S. Duval,
after a painting by A. Hoffy,
Philadelphia, 1844.
Prints and Photographs Division
(LC-USZ62-54596).

The black churches were graced by eloquent female preachers from their earliest days, although there was, as in the white churches, resistance in many quarters to the idea of women preaching the Gospel.

could not be contained, forceful black leaders followed what was becoming an American habit of forming new denominations. In 1816, for example, Richard Allen (1760–1831) and his colleagues in Philadelphia broke away from the Methodist Church and founded the African Methodist Episcopal Church, which, along with independent black Baptist congregations, flourished as the century progressed. By 1846, the A.M.E. Church, which began with eight clergy and five churches, had grown to 776 clergy, 296 churches, and 17,375 members.

Another distinctive religious group, the Mormons, arose during the period of the revivals in New York's Burned Over District. The founder of the Church of Jesus Christ of Latter-Day Saints, to give the Mormons their proper name, Joseph Smith (1805–1844), had "experienced revival preaching"—who could have avoided it in western New York in the 1820s?—and many of his followers had been "seared but not consumed" by the exuberant evangelicalism of the era.[32] Yet the Mormon church cannot be considered as a product of revivalism or as a splintering off from an existing Protestant denomination. It was *sui generis*, inspired by what Smith described as revelations on a series of gold plates, which he translated and published as the *Book of Mormon* in 1830. After numerous difficulties, including Smith's murder, the Mormons moved across the continent to Utah and developed into a major American religion.

Among the many similarities, noted above, between the revivalism of the 1740s and of the early nineteenth century, there was one pronounced difference: a political consciousness in the nineteenth century that was absent earlier. Jonathan Edwards and Gilbert Tennent expected conversion to change a person's social conduct—to alter "men's tempers and lives"[33]—but they had no political agenda and would have bridled at the idea that the purpose of changing the lives of their audiences was to promote the political prosperity of the state. Nineteenth-century evangelists, however, saw no contradiction between their roles as preachers and political activists. They were proud citizens of the new American republic and subscribed without reservation to the Founders' conviction that religion was necessary for the preservation of republican government.

Nineteenth-century evangelical literature abounds with statements that could have been inspired by the religion section of Washington's Farewell Address or copied from the Massachusetts Constitution of 1780: "the religion of the Gospel is the rock on which civil liberty rests"; "civil liberty has ever been in proportion to the prevalence of

Shakers near Lebanon state of N York, their mode of worship. **Stipple and line engraving, drawn from life. Prints and Photographs Division (LC-USZ62-13659).**

One of the distinctive features of the Shaker mode of worship was their dancing which they sometimes performed in concentric circles.

pure Christianity"; "genuine Religion with all its moral influences, and all its awful sanctions, is the chief, if not the only security we can have, for the preservation of our free institutions"; "the doctrines of Protestant Christianity are the sure, nay, the only bulwark of civil freedom"; "Christianity is the conservator of all that is dear in civil liberty and human happiness."[34] Evangelical petitions to Congress hammered away at these themes. One from a Vermont group in 1830 asserted, in the language of 1776, that "No Republican form of Government . . . can long exist in its original purity, without virtue & intelligence in the body politic . . . the principles and practice of the Christian Religion, unshackled by government, are the most effectual means of promoting & preserving that virtue and intelligence." To clinch their case, the pious petitioners added a paraphrase of Washington's Farewell Address.[35]

For the evangelical community, the way to put these convictions into action, the means of becoming "doers of the word," was, of course, the promotion of revivals. "The preservation of our invaluable liberties and free institutions and all the happy prospects of our most favored country," wrote an evangelical spokesman in 1833, "depend greatly, under God, upon those pure and frequent and spreading revivals of religion, for which all American Christians of whatever names, should pray."[36] Here was the nineteenth century's corollary to the Founder's syllogism; not simply religion, but revivals of religion, were necessary for the preservation of republican government.

As they had done earlier among the Baptists in Virginia, revivals proved their mettle in reforming social behavior in Kentucky and along the southern seaboard. A teacher traveling to Kentucky in 1802, at the peak of the revivals, was amazed at the transformation in what had been a brutal, lawless society: "I found Kentucky the most moral place I had

ever been in," wrote the teacher, "a religious awe seemed to pervade the country."[37] In South Carolina the same result was observed: "Drunkards have become sober and orderly—bruisers, bullies and blackguards meek, inoffensive and peaceable."[38] The challenge to revivalism became more formidable, however, with the acquisition of Louisiana in 1803 and with the rapid growth of urban America. Haunted for decades by the supposedly corrosive spiritual effects of western expansion, American religious leaders after 1803 saw beyond the Alleghenies an endless breeding ground for "violent and barbaric" passions. Two missionaries who traveled to the farthest reaches of the Louisiana territory in 1812 described their trip as an excursion into a moral "Valley of the Shadow of Death."[39] The nation's growing cities were another source of anxiety, for they appeared to be filling up with a coarse rabble that might be indigestible by the nation's institutions. Evangelical religion alone seemed capable of implanting into these potentially dangerous populations that portion of virtue and morality needed to sustain a republican society and government. The evangelical community, therefore, expanded its objective from the conversion of souls to the creation of citizens, the first to produce the second.

To accomplish this goal, many of the nation's denominations surmounted tensions with the evangelical camp, pooled their resources, and created institutions new to the country: the benevolent societies that, during the second decade of the nineteenth century, began to blanket the land. These societies, which one scholar has called an "evangelical united front,"[40] were inspired by British examples and were the direct result of the extraordinary energies generated by the evangelical movement, specifically by the "activism" resulting from conversion.[41] "The evidence of God's grace," Finney insisted, "was a person's benevolence toward others."[42]

Martyrdom of Joseph and Hiram Smith in Carthage Jail, June 27, 1844.
Tinted lithograph by Nagel & Weingartner, after C. G. Crehen, New York, 1851.
Prints and Photographs Division (LC-USZC4-4562).

The murder of Joseph Smith and his brother by a mob in Carthage, Illinois, prompted the Mormons, under the leadership of Brigham Young, to migrate in 1846–47 to Utah, where they found a permanent home. Although accounts differ, Smith was apparently shot to death by a mob, one of whose members then approached him with the intention, which was thwarted, of beheading him.

Grounded in the churches, the benevolent societies usually operated as independent, incorporated, ecumenical entities. Although some of the later societies were social welfare organizations, the earliest and most important ones were devoted to the conversion of souls or to the creation of conditions (sobriety sought by temperance societies) in which conversions could occur. The six largest societies in 1826–27 (based on their operating budgets) were all directly focused on conversion: the American Education Society, the American Board of Foreign Missions, the American Bible Society, the American Sunday-School Union, the American Tract Society, and the American Home Missionary Society. Three of these groups subsidized evangelical ministers, one specialized in evangelical education, and two supplied the literature that the other four used. The activity of these societies was feverish: during its first decade the American Tract Society published and distributed 35 million tracts and books; in 1836 alone, the American Sunday-School Union distributed 73 million pages of literature; by 1826 the American Bible Society was publishing three hundred thousand bibles per year; and by 1831 the American Home Missionary Society had 463 ministers in the field.[43] So great was this pulsing energy that it extorted from a hostile observer, the Scottish freethinker Fanny Wright (1795–1852), a backhanded compliment on the success of the societies in "clothing and feeding travelling preachers, who fill your streets and highways with trembling fanatics, and your very forests with frantic men and hysterical women."[44]

It is no coincidence that the years 1810–30, in which the benevolent societies were founded and generated their maximum energy, also witnessed the expiration in America of government financial support for religion. The New England states, where the practice persisted, gradually abolished it during the first decades of the nineteenth century. Massachusetts held out until 1833, when its voters terminated tax support for religion, signaling the disappearance in the United States of the ancient concept of the state as "nursing father" of the church. The task of the formation of republican citizens was now transferred to the benevolent societies—a transaction that can be called the privatization of character building. Henceforth in the United States the moral foundation of citizenship would be the responsibility of the private organizations and the churches themselves, a responsibility that the churches, bred on the revolutionary idea of being in "sweet harmony" with the state, eagerly assumed.

The benevolent societies and their supporting denominations were proud that they had assumed the double role of supporting church and country; in fact, many were boastful about what they called the patriotic dimension of their work, using the term patriotism in its literal sense of preserving the nation and its institutions. Consider the promotional literature distributed in 1826 by the American Home Missionary Society, whose records contain massive descriptions of the revivals conducted by its agents in the West and elsewhere. In 1826 the Society described how "feelings of Christian patriotism [were] excited and rendered ardent by the spiritual desolations which are seen to pervade many

Family handing out tracts.
Title page woodcut by Anderson in
***The American Tract Magazine*, August 1825.**
American Tract Society, Garland, Texas.

The American Tract Society, founded in 1825, was one of the most influential of the scores of benevolent societies that flourished in the United States in the first decades of the nineteenth century. The Tract Society, through the efforts of thousands of members like the family shown here, distributed hundreds of thousands of evangelical pamphlets, aimed at converting their recipients.

The Floating Church of Our Saviour, For Seamen
Built New York Feb. 15th, 1844, on a deck of
76 by 36 feet covering two Boats of 80 tons each
and 10 feet apart . . . permanently moored at
the foot of Pike Street. East River N.Y. Steel engraving.
Prints and Photographs Division (LC-USZ61-1258).

*Missionary societies in nineteenth-century America left no stone
unturned or no place unattended to convert their fellow Americans. This church was built by the Young Men's Church Missionary Society of New York to minister to the visiting seamen. A
floating church, built to a similar design, was moored on the
Philadelphia waterfront.*

portions of our land." "More, much more," it asserted, "must be done by the sons of the Pilgrims and
the servants of God, in the work of patriotism and
Mercy." Make no mistake, the Society assured its
readers, "we are doing the work of patriotism no
less than Christianity and the friends of civil liberty
may unite with all Christians and with the angels of
mercy in blessing God for the agency of the Society.
It has sought and, to no inconsiderable extent, it
has already promoted, that intelligence and virtue
without which civil liberty can not be maintained."[45]

A few years later a convocation of Episcopal
clergymen received the same message from one of
their spokesmen: "we owe it to patriotism as well
as piety to keep the [missionary] system . . . should
it cease . . . corruption and disorder will run riot
over our country to the destruction of our civil and
religious liberties . . . we must go forward for our
country's sake as well as that of the church."[46] Scripture was marshalled to support the synthesis of piety
and patriotism; the apostle Paul, claimed a minister,
was "one of the sublimest examples of patriotism
ever exhibited to the world." But he was, another
preacher pointed out, merely following the example
of his Master, for "Jesus Christ was a patriot."[47]

Missionary revivalism could support patriotism
in other ways, its supporters contended. One was
knitting together a society that seemed to show
signs of fragmenting, a task that many feared was
beyond the capacity of the weak, states-rights ori-
ented government of the early republic. To Lyman
Beecher (1795–1863), who believed that "every
man must be a revival man," "the prevalence of pious, intelligent, enterprising ministers throughout
the nation, at the rate of one for a thousand, would
establish . . . habits and institutions of homoge-
neous influence. These would produce a sameness
of views, and feeling, and interests which would lay

the foundation of our empire upon a rock. Religion is the central attraction which must supply that deficiency of political efficiency and interest."[48] It is worth noting that, in the last year of his life (1836), James Madison agreed with Beecher about the unifying effects of religion. "The 4 great religious sects," Madison predicted, "running through all the States, will oppose an event placing parts of each under separate Governments."[49] Religion, in short, continued to be commended as the "cement of civil society."

In the first decades of the nineteenth century evangelical America regarded itself (and was accepted by the nation's political establishment) as a voluntary partner of a weak national government, operating in an area that was constitutionally off-limits—the formation of a national character sufficiently virtuous to sustain republican government—and in an area where the federal government was politically hamstrung—the creation of national unity. Saving souls, it was thought, would save the republic. This conviction commanded a consensus that extended from the floors of Congress to the nation's cities and farms to the humble colporteur tracking through the western wilderness with a saddlebag full of bibles: all agreed that there must, as a sermon in 1826 proposed, be an "association between Religion and Patriotism."[50]

In the mid-1830s, two observers, Charles Coffin and Alexis de Tocqueville (1805–1859), commented on the role of religion in the United States in a way that summarized developments over the past two centuries. Reverend Coffin, a New England-bred minister who followed a call to preach the gospel in Tennessee, is as obscure as Tocqueville is famous, but he was a thoughtful man who knew his country's history well. In 1833 he explained why the United States had been so hospitable to evangelicalism in general and revivalism in particular:

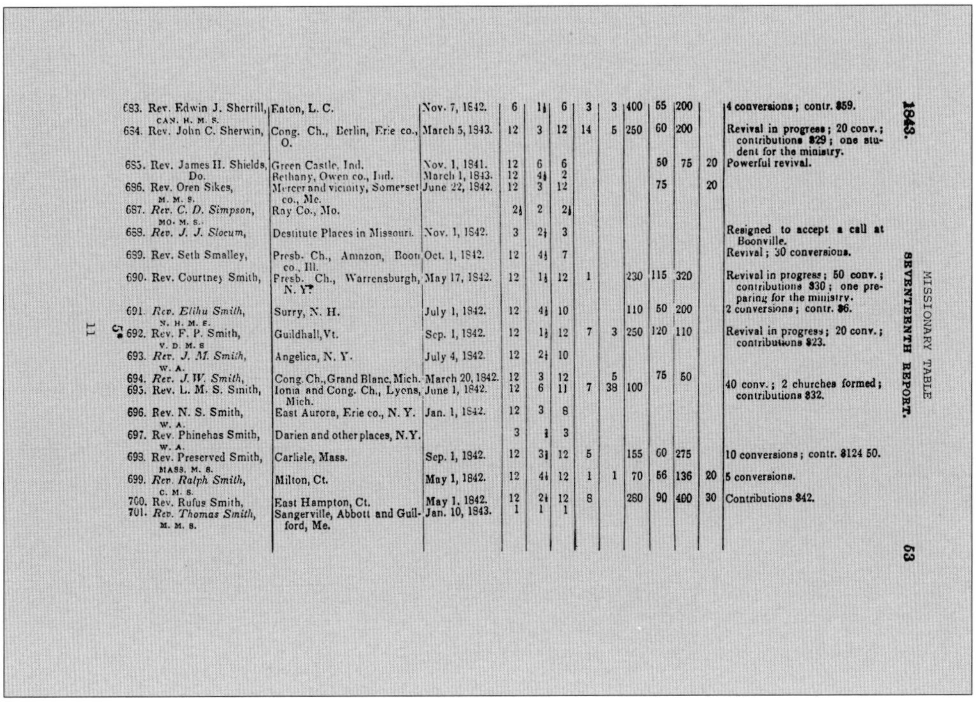

1843. SEVENTEENTH REPORT. MISSIONARY TABLE 53

683. Rev. Edwin J. Sherrill, CAN. H. M. S.	Eaton, L. C.	Nov. 7, 1842.	6	1½	6	3	3	400	55	200		4 conversions; contr. $59.
684. Rev. John C. Sherwin,	Cong. Ch., Berlin, Erie co., O.	March 5, 1843.	12	3	12	14	5	250	60	200		Revival in progress; 20 conv.; contributions $29; one student for the ministry.
685. Rev. James H. Shields,	Green Castle, Ind.	Nov. 1, 1841.	12	6	6				50	75	20	Powerful revival.
Do.	Bethany, Owen co., Ind.	March 1, 1843.	12	4½	2							
686. Rev. Oren Sikes, M. M. S.	Mercer and vicinity, Somerset co., Me.	June 22, 1842.	12	3	12				75		20	
687. *Rev. C. D. Simpson,* MO. M. S.	Ray Co., Mo.		2½	2	2½							
688. *Rev. J. J. Slocum,*	Destitute Places in Missouri.	Nov. 1, 1842.	3	2¼	3							Resigned to accept a call at Boonville.
689. Rev. Seth Smalley,	Presb. Ch., Amazon, Boon co., Ill.	Oct. 1, 1842.	12	4½	7							Revival; 30 conversions.
690. Rev. Courtney Smith,	Presb. Ch., Warrensburgh, N. Y.	May 17, 1842.	12	1½	12	1		230	115	320		Revival in progress; 50 conv.; contributions $30; one preparing for the ministry.
691. *Rev. Elihu Smith,* N. H. M. S.	Surry, N. H.	July 1, 1842.	12	4½	10			110	50	200		2 conversions; contr. $6.
692. Rev. F. P. Smith, V. D. M. S.	Guildhall, Vt.	Sep. 1, 1842.	12	1½	12	7	3	250	120	110		Revival in progress; 20 conv.; contributions $23.
693. *Rev. J. M. Smith,* W. A.	Angelica, N. Y.	July 4, 1842.	12	2¼	10							
694. *Rev. J. W. Smith,*	Cong. Ch., Grand Blanc, Mich.	March 20, 1842.	12	3	12		5		75	50		
695. Rev. L. M. S. Smith,	Ionia and Cong. Ch., Lyons, Mich.	June 1, 1842.	12	6	11	7	38	100				40 conv.; 2 churches formed; contributions $32.
696. Rev. N. S. Smith, W. A.	East Aurora, Erie co., N. Y.	Jan. 1, 1842.	12	3	8							
697. Rev. Phinehas Smith, W. A.	Darien and other places, N.Y.		3	¾	3							
698. Rev. Preserved Smith, MASS. M. S.	Carlisle, Mass.	Sep. 1, 1842.	12	3½	12	5		155	60	275		10 conversions; contr. $124 50.
699. *Rev. Ralph Smith,* C. M. S.	Milton, Ct.	May 1, 1842.	12	4½	12	1	1	70	56	136	20	5 conversions.
700. Rev. Rufus Smith,	East Hampton, Ct.	May 1, 1842.	12	2½	12	8		280	90	400	30	Contributions $42.
701. *Rev. Thomas Smith,* M. M. S.	Sangerville, Abbott and Guilford, Me.	Jan. 10, 1843.	1	1	1							

11 5*

***Missionary Table. Seventeenth Report, 1843.* American Home Missionary Society pamphlet. American Home Missionary Society Papers, Manuscript Division (LCMS-59030-1).**

A report from the Society's missionaries on revivals in progress in 1843 under their auspices.

Never was there any other country settled, since Canaan itself, so much for the sacred purposes of religion, as our own. Never did any other ancestry, since the days of inspiration, send up so many prayers and lay such ample foundations for the religious prosperity of their descendants, as did our godly forefathers. It is a fact, therefore, in perfect analogy with the course of Providence, that there never has been any other country so distinguished for religious revivals as our own.[51]

At the same time that Coffin made this observation, Tocqueville was writing up an account of his recent travels in the land of revivals that, when published in 1835 under the title *Democracy in America*, became an instant classic. Everywhere he went in America, Tocqueville encountered the conviction, fostered by the evangelical juggernaut, that for the United States to prosper there must be "an association between religion and patriotism." Tocqueville, who rarely missed a trick, perceived the importance of this idea, although he was not, apparently, aware of its Revolutionary-era roots. He recorded it with his customary clarity:

I do not know whether all the Americans have a sincere faith in their religion; for who can search the human heart? but I am certain that they hold it to be indispensable to the maintenance of republican institutions. This opinion is not peculiar to a class of citizens or to a party, but it belongs to the whole nation, and to every rank of society.[52]

232

from all trammels, they would very shortly become the most daring innovators and the most implacable disputants in the world. But the revolutionists of America are obliged to profess an ostensible respect for Christian morality and equity, which does not easily permit them to violate the laws that oppose their designs; nor would they find it easy to surmount the scruples of their partisans, even if they were able to get over their own. Hitherto no one, in the United States, has dared to advance the maxim, that everything is permissible with a view to the interests of society; an impious adage, which seems to have been invented in an age of freedom to shelter all the tyrants of future ages. Thus whilst the law permits the Americans to do what they please, religion prevents them from conceiving, and forbids them to commit what is rash or unjust.

Religion in America takes no direct part in the government of society, but it must nevertheless be regarded as the foremost of the political institutions of that country; for if it does not impart a taste for freedom, it facilitates the use of free institutions. Indeed, it is in this same point of view that the inhabitants of the United States themselves look upon religious belief. I do not know whether all the Americans have a sincere faith in their religion; for who can search the human heart? but I am certain that they hold it to be indispensable to the maintenance of republican institutions. This

233

opinion is not peculiar to a class of citizens or to a party, but it belongs to the whole nation, and to every rank of society.

In the United States, if a political character attacks a sect, this may not prevent even the partisans of that very sect from supporting him; but if he attacks all the sects together, every one abandons him, and he remains alone.

Whilst I was in America, a witness, who happened to be called at the Assizes of the county of Chester, (State of New York,) declared that he did not believe in the existence of God, or in the immortality of the soul. The judge refused to admit his evidence, on the ground that the witness had destroyed beforehand all the confidence of the Court in what he was about to say[1]. The newspapers related the fact without any further comment.

The Americans combine the notions of Christianity and of liberty so intimately in their minds, that it is impossible to make them conceive the one

[1] The New York Spectator of August 23, 1831, relates the fact in the following terms: " The Court of Common Pleas of Chester County (New York) a few days since rejected a witness who declared his disbelief in the existence of God. The presiding judge remarked, that he had not before been aware that there was a man living who did not believe in the existence of God; that this belief constituted the sanction of all testimony in a court of justice; and that he knew of no cause in a Christian country, where a witness had been permitted to testify without such belief."

Alexis de Tocqueville, *Democracy in America*, Vol. II, page 232. Translated by Henry Reeve (London, 1835). Rare Book and Special Collections Division.

Tocqueville writes here on the attitude of Americans toward religion: "I am certain that they hold it to be indispensable to the maintenance of republican institutions."

NOTES ❧

CHAPTER ONE

1. G. K. Chesterton, *What I Saw in America*, in George J. Marlin, Richard Rabatin, John L. Swan, eds., *Collected Works of G. K. Chesterton*, vols. 1–35 (San Francisco: Ignatius Press, 1986–), 21, 45.

2. Robert Browne, *Reformation without Tarrying for any* (London, 1583).

3. Perry Miller, *Errand into the Wilderness* (Cambridge: Harvard University Press, 1956), 14.

4. The victim was Alexander Leighton. *Dictionary of National Biography*, XI, 880.

5. Godfrey Davies, *The Early Stuarts 1603–1660* (Oxford: Oxford University Press, 1959), 75–6.

6. Thomas Shepard, "A Defense of the Answer," in Perry Miller and Thomas Johnson, eds., *The Puritans* (New York: American Book Company, 1938), 121.

7. John Winthrop, "A Modell of Christian Charity," ibid., 199.

8. David Hall, *The Faithful Shepherd* (Chapel Hill: University of North Carolina Press, 1972), 86.

9. Timothy Breen, *The Character of the Good Ruler* (New Haven: Yale University Press, 1970), 98.

10. Miller and Johnson, *The Puritans*, 185.

11. Perry Miller, *Orthodoxy in Massachusetts, 1630–1650* (New York: Harper & Row, 1970), 262.

12. Breen, *Good Ruler*, 40.

13. Sydney Ahlstrom, *A Religious History of the American People* (New Haven: Yale University Press, 1972), 167.

14. Patricia Bonomi, *Under the Cope of Heaven* (New York: Oxford University Press, 1986), 20.

15. Ibid., 35.

16. Jacob Marcus, *The Colonial American Jew*, 3 vols. (Detroit: Wayne State University Press, 1970), 1, 217–233.

17. William Penn to James Harrison, August 25, 1681, Richard Dunn, ed., *The Papers of William Penn*, 5 vols. (Philadelphia: University of Pennsylvania Press, 1981–87), 2, 108.

18. George Keith to Society for the Propagation of the Gospel, November 29, 1702, SPG records, series A, vol. 1, Manuscript Division (hereinafter MSS), Library of Congress (hereinafter LC).

19. Joseph Ilick, "Quakerism," Jacob E. Cooke, ed., *Encyclopedia of the North American Colonies,* 3 vols. (New York: Charles Scribner's Sons, 1993), 3, 595.

20. John Talbot to Mr. Gillingham, April 10, 1703, SPG records, MSS, LC.

21. Daniel J. Boorstin, *The Americans: The Colonial Experience* (New York: Random House, 1958), 38.

22. George Keith to Thomas Bray, February 24, 1703, SPG records, MSS, LC.

23. Citations are from William Penn's *The Frame of Government and Laws agreed upon in England*, Rare Book and Special Collections Division (hereinafter RBSCD), LC.

24. Westmoreland County, petition to Virginia General Assembly, November 2, 1785, Library of Virginia, Richmond.

25. Leo Schelbert, *Swiss Migration to America: the Swiss Mennonites* (New York: Arno Press, 1980), 151.

26. Perry Miller, *Errand*, 125n.

27. William I. Hull, *William Penn and the Dutch Quaker Migration to Pennsylvania* (Baltimore: Genealogical Publishing Company, 1970), 200.

28. Sally Schwartz, *A Mixed Multitude* (New York: New York University Press, 1987), 85.

29. Jon Butler, "Protestant Pluralism," *Encyc. North American Colonies*, 3, 619.

30. Patricia Bonomi, "Religious Dissent and the Case for American Exceptionalism," Ronald Hoffman and Peter Albert, eds., *Religion in a Revolutionary Age* (Charlottesville: University Press of Virginia, 1994), 38, 44.

31. Charles McLean Andrews, *The Colonial Period in American History*, 4 vols. (New Haven: Yale University Press, 1934–38), 2, 279.

32. Ibid., 291.

33. James Hennesey, "Roman Catholicism: The British and Dutch Colonies," *Encyc. North American Colonies*, 3, 555.

34. Copy in Law Library, Library of Congress.

35. Parke Rouse, *James Blair of Virginia* (Chapel Hill: University of North Carolina, 1971), 57.

36. George MacLaren Brydon, *Virginia's Mother Church and the Political Conditions under which it grew*, 2 vols. (Richmond: Virginia Historical Society, 1947–52), 1, 486.

37. Miller, *Errand*, 132.

38. Ibid., 101.

39. Ibid.

40. John Smith, *Advertisements for the unexperienced Planters of New-England*, Edward Arber, ed., *Works of Captain John Smith* (New York: AMS Press, 1967), 957.

41. Miller, *Errand*, 104.

42. Ibid., 105.

43. William W. Hening, *The Statutes at Large . . . of Virginia*, 13 vols. (Charlottesville: University Press of Virginia, 1969), 1, 180.

44. Paul L. Ford, ed., Thomas Jefferson, *Notes on the State of Virginia* (Brooklyn: Historical Printing Club, 1894), 195–6.

45. Jon Butler, *Awash in a Sea of Faith: Christianizing the American People* (Cambridge: Harvard University Press, 1990), 49–50.

46. Brydon, *Virginia's Mother Church*, 491.

47. John Frederick Woolverton, "Anglicanism," *Encyc. North American Colonies*, 3, 566.

CHAPTER TWO

1. Butler, *Awash*, 2; Bonomi, *Cope of Heaven*, 6; Marilyn Westerkamp, *The Triumph of the Laity: Scots-Irish Piety and the Great Awakening 1625–1760* (New York: Oxford University Press, 1988), 10.

2. John Talbot to SPG, April 7, 1704; John Thomas to SPG, June 27, 1705; SPG records, MSS, LC.

3. Patricia Bonomi and Peter Eisenstadt, "Church Adherence in the Eighteenth-Century British American Colonies," *William and Mary Quarterly*, 3rd series, 31 (April 1982), 247.

4. Ahlstrom, *Religious History*, 211–12.

5. Perry Miller, *The New England Mind: From Colony to Province* (Cambridge: Harvard University Press, 1953), 34–6.

6. Breen, *Good Ruler*, 105.

7. Robert Pope, "New England versus the New England Mind: the Myth of Declension," *Journal of Social History*, 3 (Winter 1969–70), 101.

8. Anne Braude, "Women's History *Is* American Religious History," in Thomas W. Tweed, ed., *Retelling U.S. Religious History* (Berkeley: University of California Press, 1997), 93.

9. Bonomi, "Religious Dissent," 41.

10. Ibid., 39.

11. Harry S. Stout, "George Whitefield in Three Countries," Mark Noll, David W. Bebbington, George A. Rawlyk, eds., *Evangelicalism* (New York: Oxford University Press, 1994), 63.

12. Bonomi, "Religious Dissent," 41.

13. For references in this paragraph, see Bonomi, "Religious Dissent," 41; Bonomi, "Church Adherence," 259, 265, 267; George Keith to SPG, April 30, 1703, SPG records, MSS, LC; Edwin S. Gaustad, *Historical Atlas of Religion in America* (New York: Harper & Row, 1962), 3.

14. See Butler, *Awash*, 37–66.

15. These figures are presented in Gaustad, *Historical Atlas*, 3.

16. Bonomi, "Church Adherence," 274.

17. Richard Bushman, ed., *The Great Awakening: Documents on the Revival of Religion* (New York: Atheneum, 1970), 129–30.

18. Ibid., 71.

19. Butler, *Awash*, 165.

20. David W. Bebbington, *Evangelicalism in Modern Britain* (London: Unwin Hyman, 1989), 1; Michael J. Crawford, *Seasons of Grace* (New York: Oxford University Press, 1991), 4.

21. Ibid., 20–21, passim.

22. Ibid., 47.

23. John Walsh, "'Methodism' and the Origins of English-Speaking Evangelicalism," Noll, ed., *Evangelicalism*, 22.

24. Bushman, *Great Awakening*, 41.

25. Ibid., 71.

26. Hall, *Faithful Shepherd*, 65.

27. Bushman, *Great Awakening*, 68.

28. On Tennent's "elocutionary reserve," see Alan Heimert, *Religion and the American Mind* (Cambridge: Harvard University Press, 1966), 229.

29. Bushman, *Great Awakening*, 122.

30. Perry Miller, *The New England Mind: The Seventeenth Century* (Cambridge: Harvard University Press, reprint ed., 1954), 28.

31. Joseph Tracy, *The Great Awakening* (New York: Arno Press, 1969), 217.

32. Bushman, *Great Awakening*, 79.

33. Ibid., 116.

34. Harry S. Stout, "George Whitefield in Three Countries," Noll, ed., *Evangelicalism*, 63.

35. Walsh, "'Methodism,'" ibid., 28.

36. Heimert, *Religion and the American Mind*, 36.

37. Harry Stout, "Religion, Communications, and the Revolution," *William and Mary Quarterly*, 3rd series, 34 (October 1977), 533.

38. Edwin S. Gaustad, *Faith of our Fathers* (San Francisco: Harper and Row, 1987), 96.

39. Stout, "Whitefield in Three Countries," Noll, *Evangelicalism*, 69.

40. Butler, *Awash*, 191.

41. Bushman, *Great Awakening*, xi.

42. Edwin S. Gaustad, *The Great Awakening in New England* (New York: Harpers, 1957), 27.

43. Ibid., 32.

44. Crawford, *Seasons of Grace*, 170.

45. Bushman, *Great Awakening*, 88.

46. David S. Lovejoy, *Religious Enthusiasm and the Great Awakening* (Englewood Cliffs, New Jersey: Prentice-Hall, 1969), 17.

47. Jon Butler, "Coercion, Miracle, Reason: Rethinking the American Religious Experience in the Revolutionary Age," Hoffman, ed., *Religion in a Revolutionary Age*, 20.

48. Edwin S. Gaustad, *Faith of our Fathers* (San Francisco: Harper & Row, 1987), 65–6.

49. Douglas Adair, "Was Alexander Hamilton a Christian Statesman?", Trevor Colbourn, ed., *Fame and the Founding Fathers* (New York: W. W. Norton, 1974), 141–59.

50. Nathan Schachner, "Alexander Hamilton viewed by his Friends: The Narratives of Robert Troup and Hercules Mulligan," *William and Mary Quarterly*, 3rd series, 4 (April 1947), 212–13.

51. Leonard Bacon, *A History of American Christianity* (New York: Christian Literature Company, 1897), 230.

52. Bonomi, "Church Adherence," 274, n.121.

53. Stephen A. Marini, "Religion, Politics and Ratification," Hoffman, ed., *Religion in a Revolutionary Age*, 188, 193.

54. Susan Juster, *Disorderly Women: Sexual Politics & Evangelicalism in Revolutionary New England* (Ithaca: Cornell University Press, 1994), 113. For another account of women during the eighteenth-century revivals, see Mary Beth Norton, "'My Resting Reaping Times': Sarah Osborne's Defense of Her 'Unfeminine Activities,'" *Signs*, 2 (1976), 515–29.

55. See Leigh Eric Schmidt, *Holy fairs: Scottish communions and American revivals in the early modern period* (Princeton: Princeton University Press, 1989).

56. Crawford, *Seasons of Grace*, 163.

57. Lyman Butterfield, "Elder John Leland, Jeffersonian Itinerant," American Antiquarian Society, *Proceedings*, 62 (October 1952), 171.

58. Ibid., 181.

59. Boorstin, *The Americans*, 135.

60. Marini, "Religion, Politics and Ratification," 198.

61. Butler, "Coercion, Miracle, Reason," 25.

62. Ahlstrom, *Religious History*, 385.

63. Butler, "Coercion," 1; John Murrin, "No Awakening, No Revolution? More Counterfactual Speculations," *Reviews in American History*, 11 (June 1983), 169.

64. Butler, *Awash*, 188.

CHAPTER THREE

1. Joseph Galloway, *Historical and Political Reflections on the Rise and Progress of the American Rebellion* (London, 1780), 54.

2. Bonomi, "Religious Dissent," 48.

3. Heimert, *Religion and the American Mind*, 12.

4. Ibid., 21.

5. Butler, "Coercion, Miracle, Reason," 9.

6. Nathan O. Hatch, "The Democratization of Christianity and the Character of American Politics," Mark Noll, ed., *Religion and American Politics* (New York: Oxford University Press, 1990), 99; Hatch, *The Democratization of American Christianity* (New Haven: Yale University Press, 1989), 82–3.

7. Heimert, *Religion and the American Mind*, 1.

8. Rodger D. Parker, *Wellsprings of a Nation* (Worcester, Mass.: American Antiquarian Society, 1977), 69.

9. Mark A. Noll, *Christians in the American Revolution* (Grand Rapids, Mich.: Christian University Press, 1977), 60.

10. Bonomi, *Cope of Heaven*, 216.

11. Elaine Forman Crane, "Religion and Rebellion: Women of Faith in the American War for Independence," Hoffman, ed., *Religion in a Revolutionary Age*, 56–7.

12. Bruce Kuklick, ed., *Political Writings of Thomas Paine* (New York: Cambridge University Press, 1989), 9.

13. Philip Foner, *The Complete Writings of Thomas Paine*, 2 vols. (New York: Citadel Press, 1945), 1, 79.

14. For representative collections of political sermons of the Revolution, see John Wingate Thornton, ed., *The Pulpit of the American Revolution* (Boston: Gould and Lincoln, 1860); Frank Moore, ed., *The Patriot Preachers of the American Revolution* (New York: privately printed, 1860); and Ellis Sandoz, ed., *Political Sermons of the American Founding Era* (Indianapolis: Liberty Press, 1991).

15. Butler, *Awash*, 201–2.

16. Leonard J. Kramer, "Muskets in the Pulpits," *Journal of the Presbyterian Historical Society*, 31 (December 1953), 229.

17. J. C. D. Clark, *The Language of Liberty, 1660–1832* (Cambridge: Cambridge University Press, 1994), 305.

18. Bonomi, *Cope of Heaven*, 205, 208–9.

19. James Smylie, *American Presbyterians: A Pictorial History* (Philadelphia: Presbyterian Historical Society, 1985), 42.

20. Noll, *Christians in the American Revolution*, 68.

21. David Holmes, "The Episcopal Church and the American Revolution," *Historical Magazine of the Protestant Episcopal Church*, 47 (September 1978), 283.

22. Noll, *Christians*, 68.

23. On millennialism during the founding period, see Ruth H. Bloch, *Visionary republic: millennial themes in American Thought* (Cambridge: Cambridge University Press, 1985).

CHAPTER FOUR

1. Thomson's Bible, published in Philadelphia by Jane Aitken, is in RBSCD, LC. Dickinson's commentaries are in his papers at the Historical Society of Pennsylvania. For Boudinot's letter to his daughter Sarah, October 30, 1782, see Paul H. Smith, et al., eds., *Letters of Delegates to Congress 1774–1789*, 25 vols. (Washington: Government Printing Office, 1976–1998), 19, 325; for Laurens, see Edmund S. Morgan, "The Puritan Ethic and the American Revolution," *William and Mary Quarterly*, 3rd series, 24 (January 1967), 29; for Jay, see entry in *Dictionary of American Biography* (DAB), 10, 5–10; Zubly is discussed in James H. Hutson, *The Sister Republics: Switzerland and the United States from 1776 to the Present* (Washington: Government Printing Office, 1991), 17–18. Galloway's *Brief commentaries upon such parts of the Revelation and other prophecies as immediately refer to the present times. . . .* (London, 1802) is in RBSCD.

2. Perry Miller, "From Covenant to Revival," James Ward Smith and A. Leland Jamison, eds., *The Shaping of American Religion* (Princeton: Princeton University Press, 1961), 330.

3. Congress issued the following fast and thanksgiving day proclamations: Fast days: June 12, 1775; March 16, 1776; December 11, 1776; March 7, 1778; March 20, 1781; March 19, 1782. Thanksgiving day proclamations: November 1, 1777; October 20, 1779; October 18, 1780; October 26, 1781; October 11, 1782; October 18, 1783; August 3, 1784. These may be consulted, under the appropriate dates, in Worthington C. Ford and Gaillard Hunt, eds., *Journals of the Continental Congress, 1774–1789*, 34 vols. (Washington: Library of Congress, 1904–37), hereinafter cited as JCC.

4. Ibid., 11, 477.

5. Smith, *Letters of Delegates*, 1, 497–8.

6. Miller, "Covenant to Revival," 325–7.

7. Miller, *The New England Mind*, 480.

8. Harry Stout, *The New England Soul: preaching and religious culture in colonial New England* (New York: Oxford University Press, 1986), 285.

9. Miller, "Covenant to Revival," 330.

10. JCC, 4, 208.

11. Ibid., 16, 252.

12. Ibid., 4, 209; 19, 285.

13. Ibid., 4, 209.

14. Ibid., 4, 209.

15. Ibid., 9, 855.

16. Ibid., 10, 229.

17. Ibid., 4, 209.

18. Ibid., 9, 855.

19. Ibid., 13, 344.

20. Smith, *Letters of Delegates*, 4, 234.

21. In RBSCD, LC.

22. Ibid.

23. JCC, 6, 1022.

24. Smith, *Letters of Delegates*, 7, 311–12.

25. Ibid., 19, 118.

26. JCC, 22, 138.

27. The Land Ordinance of 1785 is in RBSCD, LC.

28. Ibid.

29. Smith, *Letters of Delegates*, 24, 404–5.

30. JCC, 22, 138.

CHAPTER FIVE

1. John Talbot to SPG, October 20, 1704; William Urquhart and John Thomas to SPG, November 14, 1705, SPG records, MSS, LC.

2. Thomas J. Curry, *The First Freedoms: Church and State in America to the Passage of the First Amendment* (New York: Oxford University Press, 1986), 97–8.

3. Proclamation, April 15, 1775, Library of Congress, RBSCD.

4. *Continental Journal*, March 9, 1780.

5. Library of Virginia, Richmond.

6. Ibid.

7. Benjamin Rush to Thomas Jefferson, August 22, 1800. Lyman H. Butterfield, ed., *Letters of Benjamin Rush*, 2 vols. (Princeton: Princeton University Press, 1951), 2, 820–21.

8. John Boles, *The Great Revival, 1787–1805: the origins of the Southern evangelical mind* (Lexington: University Press of Kentucky, 1972), 176.

9. Charles Keller, *The Second Great Awakening in Connecticut* (Hamden, Conn.: Anchor Books, 1968), 148.

10. Oscar Handlin, ed., *Popular Sources of Political Authority: Documents on the Massachusetts Constitution of 1780* (Cambridge: Harvard University Press, 1966), 764.

11. *Boston Gazette*, November 27, 1780.

12. Nathan Williams, *A Sermon preached on the Audience of the General Assembly of the State of Connecticut* (Hartford, 1780), 14.

13. Petition to General Assembly, November 14, 1785, Library of Virginia, Richmond.

14. Paul A. Rahe, *Republics Ancient and Modern* (Chapel Hill: University of North Carolina Press, 1992), 749.

15. Ibid., 751.

16. Library of Virginia, Richmond.

17. Rahe, *Republics*, 749.

18. Curry, *First Freedoms*, 153.

19. Gaustad, *Faith of our Fathers*, 171.

20. Curry, *First Freedoms*, 155; the statute is printed in a broadside, January 12, 1785, RBSCD, LC.

21. Rockingham County, petition, December 1, 1784, to Virginia General Assembly, J. H. Eckenrode, *Separation of Church and State in Virginia* (New York: Da Capo Press, 1971), 97.

22. James Hennesey, "Roman Catholicism: British and Dutch," *Encyc. North American Colonies*, 3, 559.

23. Surry County, petition to Virginia General Assembly, November 14, 1785, Library of Virginia, Richmond.

24. A copy of Henry's bill is in the Washington Papers, December 24, 1784, MSS, LC.

25. Washington to Mason, October 3, 1785, in Robert Rutland, ed., *The Papers of George Mason*, 3 vols. (Chapel Hill: University of North Carolina Press, 1970), 2, 831–2.

26. Fred J. Hood, *Reformed America: The Middle and Southern States 1783–1837* (University, Alabama: University Press of Alabama, 1980), 18.

27. The Hanover Presbytery petition is in the Library of Virginia. For Alison, see James L. McAllister, Jr., "Francis Alison and John Witherspoon: Political Philosophers and Revolutionaries," *Journal of Presbyterian History* 54 (Spring 1976), 44.

28. Butterfield, "Elder John Leland," 164.

29. William McLoughlin, *Isaac Backus and the American Pietistic Tradition* (Boston: Little, Brown and Company, 1967), 136; McLoughlin, "The Role of Religion in the Revolution," Stephen F. Kurtz and James H. Hutson, eds., *Essays on the American Revolution* (Chapel Hill: University of North Carolina Press, 1973), 212.

30. "Several Baptist Associations," assembled in Powhatan County, petition, August 13, 1785, to Virginia General Assembly, Library of Virginia.

31. McLoughlin, *Isaac Backus*, 139–140.

32. *Boston Gazette*, November 2, 1778.

33. McLoughlin, *Isaac Backus*, 150.

34. *Continental Journal*, May 18, 1780; *Boston Gazette*, November 2, 1778.

35. Westmoreland County, petition, November 2, 1785, to Virginia General Assembly, Library of Virginia.

36. Petition of "Several Baptist Associations," August 13, 1785.

37. Hanover Presbytery, petition, October 24, 1776, to Virginia General Assembly, Library of Virginia.

38. Westmoreland County, petition, November 2, 1785.

39. The quotations in this paragraph are from Rhys Isaac, "Evangelical Revolt: The Nature of the Baptists' Challenge to the Traditional Order in Virginia, 1765 to 1775," *William and Mary Quarterly*, 3rd series, 31 (July 1974), 353–4, 358.

40. Rahe, *Republics*, 758.

41. John Murrin, "Religion and Politics in America from the First Settlements to the Civil War," Noll, ed., *Religion and American Politics*, 32.

42. Donald Lutz and Jack Warren, *A Covenanted People: The Religious Tradition and the Origins of American Constitutionalism* (Providence: The John Carter Brown Library, 1987), 63.

43. Robert Rutland, ed., *The Papers of James Madison*, 18 vols. (Chicago: University of Chicago Press and Charlottesville: University Press of Virginia, 1962), 8, 198.

44. Ibid., 303.

45. Jefferson, *Notes on Virginia*, 199.

46. Julian P. Boyd, ed., *The Papers of Thomas Jefferson*, 27 vols. (Princeton: Princeton University Press, 1950-), 2, 545–7; see also Merrill Peterson, ed., *The Virginia Statute for Religious Freedom: its evolution and consequences in American history* (Cambridge: Cambridge University Press, 1988).

47. Westmoreland County, petition, November 2, 1785, to Virginia General Assembly. For a searching study of the church-state debate in revolutionary Virginia, see Thomas E. Buckley, *Church and State in Revolutionary Virginia, 1776–1787* (Charlottesville: University Press of Virginia, 1977).

48. Gordon Wood, *The Creation of the American Republic* (Chapel Hill: University of North Carolina Press, 1968), 427; McLoughlin, "Role of Religion in the Revolution," 222.

49. On the Supreme Court's use of the Virginia assessment controversy, see Daniel L. Dreisbach, "Thomas Jefferson and Bills Number 82–86 of the Revision of the Laws of Virginia, 1776–1786: New Light on the Jeffersonian Model of Church-State Relations," *The North Carolina Law Review*, 69 (November 1990), 171–78.

CHAPTER SIX

1. David Hawke, *Benjamin Rush: revolutionary gadfly* (Indianapolis: Bobbs-Merrill, 1971), 357.

2. Harry S. Stout, "Rhetoric and Reality in the Early Republic: The Case of the Federalist Clergy," Noll, ed., *Religion and American Politics*, 62–3.

3. JCC, 19, 285.

4. Max Farrand, ed., *The Records of the Federal Convention*, 4 vols. (New Haven: Yale University Press, 1937), 1, 451–2.

5. Edmund C. Burnett, *The Continental Congress* (New York: Macmillan, 1941), 38.

6. Rahe, *Republics Ancient and Modern*, 1123n.

7. RBSCD, LC.

8. Butterfield, "Elder John Leland," 188, 195.

9. Rutland, ed., *Papers of James Madison*, 12, 201.

10. The "Detached Memoranda" is in the Rives Papers, MSS, LC. For a printed version, see Elizabeth Fleet, ed., "Madison's 'Detached Memoranda,'" *William and Mary Quarterly*, 3rd series, 3 (1946), 534–62.

11. RBSCD, LC.

12. *Annals of Congress* (Washington: Gales and Seaton, 1834), 1, 913.

13. Ibid., 914.

14. Ibid., 914.

15. John C. Fitzpatrick, ed., *The Writings of George Washington*, 39 vols. (Washington: Government Printing Office, 1931–44), 30, 427–8.

16. Ibid., 31, 93n.

17. Ibid., 26, 496.

18. Ibid., 35, 229.

19. Gaustad, *Faith of our Fathers*, 93.

20. Ibid., 92.

21. Rahe, *Republics*, 1122n.

22. James D. Richardson, ed., *A Compilation of the Messages and Papers of the Presidents, 1789–1897*, 10 vols. (Washington: Government Printing Office, 1896–99), 1, 259.

23. Fred Hood, *Reformed America: The Middle and Southern States, 1783–1837* (University, Alabama: The University Press of Alabama, 1980), 104.

24. Richardson, *Compilation*, 274–5.

25. *Notes on the State of Virginia*, 197.

26. Quoted in Eugene Sheridan, "Liberty and Virtue: Religion and Republicanism in Jeffersonian Thought," unpublished paper in the author's possession, 31.

27. Paul K. Conkin, "Priestley and Jefferson, Unitarianism as a Religion for a New Revolutionary Age," Hoffman, ed., *Religion in a Revolutionary Age*, 293, 301.

28. Dickinson W. Adams, ed., *Jefferson's Extracts from the Gospels* (Princeton: Princeton University Press, 1983), 331.

29. Edwin S. Gaustad, *Sworn on the Altar of God: A Religious Biography of Thomas Jefferson* (Grand Rapids, Mich.: William B. Eerdmans Publishing Company, 1996), 124.

30. Conkin, "Priestley and Jefferson," 293; Gaustad, *Sworn on the Altar*, x, xiii.

31. Sheridan, "Liberty and Virtue," 23.

32. Gaustad, *Sworn on the Altar*, 119.

33. Both the "Philosophy of Jesus of Nazareth" and "The Life and Morals of Jesus" can be conveniently consulted in Adams, *Jefferson's Extracts*.

34. Sheridan, "Liberty and Virtue," 37.

35. Gaustad, *Sworn on the Altar*, 135.

36. Ibid., 139.

37. Gaillard Hunt, ed., *The first forty years of Washington society* (New York: Charles Scribner's Sons, 1906), 13.

38. Manasseh Cutler to Josiah Torrey, January 3, 1803, William Parker Cutler and Julia Perkins Cutler, eds., *Life Journals and Correspondence of Rev. Manasseh Cutler, LL.D.*, 2 vols. (Athens: Ohio University Press, 1987), 2, 119.

39. Catharine Mitchill to Margaret Miller, April 8, 1806, Carolyn H. Sung, "Catharine Mitchill's Letters from Washington 1806–1812," *Quarterly Journal of the Library of Congress*, 34 (July 1977), 175.

40. Thomas Claggett to James Kemp, February 18, 1801, Maryland Diocesan Archives. Church services in the Capitol may have begun five years earlier. Wilhelmus B. Bryan, a pioneering but conscientious historian of Washington, D.C., mentions an item in the city's first newspaper (of which only a few copies are extant), the *Impartial Observer and Washington Advertiser*, June 19, 1795, which indicates that the Capitol, though still in its initial stages of construction, was used for religious observances of some sort. Wilhelmus B. Bryan, "The Beginnings of the Presbyterian Church in the District of Columbia," *Records of the Columbia Historical Society*, 8 (1905), 54.

41. Hunt, ed., *Washington Society*, 13.

42. Everett O. Alldredge, *Centennial History of First Congregational United Church of Christ Washington, D.C.* (Baltimore: Port City Press, 1965), 10.

43. A. P. C. Griffin, "Issues of the Press in 1800–1802," *Records of the Columbia Historical Society*, 4 (1901), 58.

44. *Alexandria Advertiser*, July 14, 1801; see also *National Intelligencer*, June 29, July 1, 1801.

45. Jefferson, Account Book, 1791–1803 (photostatic copy), June 25, 1801, MSS, LC. Jefferson also gave Austin twenty-five dollars "in charity" on November 2, 1801, and again on May 1, 1802. Ibid. It should be noted that Austin was one of the few New England-bred Congregational ministers who supported Jefferson in the election of 1800.

46. Abijah Bigelow to Hannah Bigelow, January 10, 1813, "Letters of Abijah Bigelow, Member of Congress, to his Wife, 1810–1815," American Antiquarian Society, *Proceedings*, 40 (1930), 353.

47. Viator (Joseph Varnum), *The Washington Sketch Book* (New York, 1864), 107.

48. Thomas H. Hubbard to Phebe Hubbard, December 17, 1821, MSS, LC.

49. Ripley describes her appearance in the House in Dorothy Ripley, *The Bank of Faith and Works United* (2nd edit., Whitby, Yorkshire: G. Clark Publisher, 1822). The tradition that Jefferson himself invited Ripley to preach in the House is apparently without foundation. See Elizabeth Muir, "The Bark Schoolhouse: Methodist Episcopal Missionary Women in Upper Canada, 1827–1833," in John S. Moir and C. T. McIntire, eds., *Canadian Protestant and Catholic Missions, 1820s–1960s* (New York: Peter Lang, 1988), 31.

50. Obituary, February 10, 1832, in *Christian Advocate and Journal and Zion's Herald*.

51. William E. Dodd, *The Life of Nathaniel Macon* (reprint ed., New York: Burt Franklin, 1970), 377.

52. For Harriet Livermore, see Catherine Brekus, "Harriet Livermore, the Pilgrim Stranger: Female Preaching and Biblical Feminism in Early-Nineteenth-Century America," *Church History* 65 (September 1996), 389–404.

53. John Fairfield to his wife, December 28, 1835, Fairfield Papers, MSS, LC.

54. Cutler, diary, February 27, 1803, *Life of Cutler*, 2, 118.

55. Abijah Bigelow to Hannah Bigelow, January 20, 1811, *Letters of Bigelow*, 314.

56. Elizabeth Murray, *Two Hundred Years ago or the Life and Times of the Rev. Walter Dulany Addison 1769–1848* (Philadelphia: George Jacobs, 1895), 147–8. See also John Quincy Adams, diary, February 5, 1804, Adams papers microfilm edition, reel 30, MSS, LC.

57. John Hargrove, *A sermon on the Second Coming of Christ, and on the last Judgment: delivered on the 25th December, 1804, before both houses of Congress, at the Capitol in the city of Washington* (Baltimore, 1805), RBSCD, LC.

58. Augustus Foster, diary, MSS, LC.

59. Hunt, ed., *Washington Society*, 16–17.

60. Ibid., 14.

61. Abijah Bigelow to Hannah Bigelow, December 28, 1812, *Letters of Bigelow*, op.cit., 349.

62. Cutler, diary, December 23, 1804, *Life of Cutler*, 2, 174.

63. Ibid., November 11, 1804, 2, 171; Adams, diary, February 2, 1806.

64. The corrected draft of the Danbury Baptist letter is in the Jefferson Papers, MSS, LC. An excellent essay, describing the context in which the Danbury letter was composed and its meaning, is Daniel L. Dreisbach, "'Sowing Useful Truths and Principles': The Danbury Baptists, Thomas Jefferson, and the 'Wall of Separation,'" *Journal of Church and State* 39 (Summer 1997), 455–501.

65. *Reynolds* v. *United States*, 98 U.S. 145, 164 (1878).

66. *Everson* v. *Board of Education*, 330 U.S. 1, 16, 18 (1947).

67. Dreisbach, "Sowing Useful Truths," 20.

68. Jefferson to Levi Lincoln, January 1, 1802, Jefferson Papers, MSS, LC.

69. Jefferson to Samuel Miller, January 23, 1808, ibid.

70. Jefferson, Danbury Baptist letter, marginal note.

71. Manasseh Cutler to Joseph Torrey, January 4, 1802, *Life of Cutler*, 2, 66, 119. Cutler meant that Jefferson attended church on January 3, 1802, for the first time *as president*. Bishop Claggett's letter of February 18, 1801, cited above, reveals that, as vice-president, Jefferson went to church services in the House. Cutler could not, of course, have known of Jefferson's church attendance in the winter of 1801, since he was not in Congress at that time.

72. Gaustad, *Sworn on the altar*, 206.

73. Entry of May 15, 1805, Account Book, 1804–1826 (photostatic copy), MSS, LC.

74. April 7, 1802, Account Book, 1791–1803; February 20, 1805, Account Book, 1804–1826.

75. March 2, 1803, Account Book, 1791–1803. For the information about Reverend Chambers I am indebted to George Combs of Lloyd House, Alexandria Public Library, Virginia.

76. April 18, 19, June 28, 1806; Account Book, 1804–1826, ibid. See also Fern C. Stukenbroeker, *A Watermelon for God: A History of Trinity United Methodist Church, Alexandria, Virginia (1774–1974)* (Alexandria: Stukenbroeker, 1974), 102.

77. For this reference, I am indebted to Margaret Shannon, who has assisted me with her encyclopedic knowledge of religion in early Washington.

78. Richard P. Jackson, *The Chronicles of Georgetown, D.C., from 1751 to 1878* (Washington: R. O. Polkinhorn, 1878), 145; Dorothy Shaffter, *The Presbyterian Church in Georgetown, 1780–1970* (Washington: Session of the Presbyterian Congregation in Georgetown, 1971), 31. See October 20, 1802, entry, Account Book, 1791–1803. For Jefferson's contribution to Laurie's church, see January 15, 1805, entry, Account Book, 1804–1826.

79. Hunt, ed., *Washington Society*, 13.

80. For McCormick, see his obituary in the *National Intelligencer*, April 28, 1841.

81. Allen's history is in the MMC Collection, 1167, MSS, LC.

82. July 2, 1804, June 3, 1805, January 6, 1807, Account Book, 1804–1826.

83. Foster, diary, MSS, LC.

84. Abijah Bigelow to Hannah Bigelow, December 28, 1812, *Letters of Bigelow*, 349.

85. Gaustad, *Sworn on the Altar*, 179.

86. Hunt, ed., *Writings of Madison*, 9, 230.

87. Rahe, *Republics*, 763.

CHAPTER SEVEN

1. Charles Cole, *The Social Ideas of Northern Evangelists* (New York: Octagon Books, 1966), 72, passim.

2. Ibid., 76.

3. Nathan Hatch, *The Democratization of American Christianity* (New Haven: Yale University Press, 1989), 261n.

4. Charles Keller, *The Second Great Awakening in Connecticut*, 2.

5. Ibid., 24.

6. Cole, *Social Ideas*, 73; Boles, *The Great Revival, 1787–1805*, 19, 41; Terry Bilhartz, *Urban Religion and the Second Great Awakening: Church and Society in early national Baltimore* (Rutherford, N.J.: Fairleigh Dickinson University Press, 1986), 85; Keller, *Second Great Awakening*, 37.

7. Cole, *Social Ideas*, 73.

8. Bilhartz, *Urban Religion*, 136.

9. Keller, *Second Great Awakening*, 15.

10. Ibid.

11. Ahlstrom, *Religious History*, 417.

12. Cole, *Social Ideas*, 75.

13. Ibid., 74.

14. Boles, *The Great Revival, 1787–1805*, 40.

15. Ibid., 65.

16. Ibid., 67.

17. Ibid., 64.

18. Westerkamp, *Triumph of the laity*, 186.

19. Daniel Cohen, *The Spirit of the Lord: revivalism in America* (New York: Four Winds Press, 1975), 19.

20. Gaustad, *The Great Awakening*, 32.

21. Cohen, *The Spirit of the Lord*, 22.

22. Boles, *The Great Revival, 1787–1805*, 89.

23. Richard Carwardine, *Trans-Atlantic Revivalism: Popular Evangelicalism in Britain and America 1790–1815* (Westport, Conn.: Greenwood Press, 1978), 12.

24. Ibid., 12.

25. Richard Carwardine, "The Second Great Awakening in the Urban Centers: An Examination of Methodism and the 'New Measures,'" *Journal of American History* 59 (September 1972), 328.

26. Carwardine, *Trans-Atlantic Revivalism*, 18.

27. Ahlstrom, *Religious History*, 437.

28. For a discussion of this point, see Mechal Sobel, *The world they made together: Black and White Values in eighteenth-century Virginia* (Princeton: Princeton University Press, 1987); readers ought also to be aware of Jon Butler's provocative argument that the enslavement and transportation of Africans to America amounted to nothing less than a "spiritual holocaust." *Awash*, 129–63.

29. Sylvia R. Frey, "'The Year of Jubilee is Come:' Black Christianity in the Plantation South in Post-Revolutionary America," *Religion in Revolutionary America*, 92.

30. Hatch, *The Democratization of American Christianity*, 102.

31. See, for example, James Essig, *The bonds of wickedness: American evangelicals against slavery, 1770–1808* (Philadelphia: Temple University Press, 1982); for a recent argument that the southern evangelicals sacrificed the interests of their black members to ingratiate themselves with local slave holding elites, see Christine Heyrman, *Southern Cross* (New York: Alfred A. Knopf, 1997).

32. Ahlstrom, *Religious History*, 503.

33. John Walsh, "'Methodism,'" Noll, *Evangelicalism*, 26.

34. Hood, *Reformed America*, 61, 63, 66; Cole, *Social Ideas*, 14, 19.

35. John G. West, Jr., *The Politics of Revelation and Reason: Religion and Civic Life in the New Nation* (Lawrence: University of Kansas, 1996), 141–2.

36. Crawford, *Seasons of Grace*, 250.

37. Boles, *The Great Revival, 1787–1805*, 93.

38. Ibid., 188.

39. Charles I. Foster, *An Errand of Mercy: The Evangelical United Front 1790–1837* (Chapel Hill: University of North Carolina Press, 1960), 184.

40. Ibid., chapter 8, passim. For the tensions in the evangelical camp, see Richard Carwardine, *Evangelicals and Politics in Antebellum America* (New Haven: Yale University Press, 1993).

41. On evangelical "activism," see Bebbington, *Evangelicalism in Modern Britain*, 10–12.

42. Clifford Griffin, *Their Brothers' Keeper: Moral Stewardship in the United States, 1800–1865* (Westport, Conn.: Greenwood Press, 1983), 48.

43. Foster, *Errand of Mercy*, 121–2, 224, passim.

44. West, *Politics of Revelation*, 135.

45. American Home Missionary Society, constitution and circular, 1826, RBSCD, LC.

46. Bilhartz, *Urban Religion and the Second Great Awakening*, 53.

47. Hood, *Reformed America*, 65.

48. Foster, *Errand of Mercy*, 57.

49. Hunt, *Writings of Madison*, 9, 610.

50. Hood, *Reformed America*, 67.

51. Crawford, *Seasons of Grace*, 249.

52. Alexis de Tocqueville, *Democracy in America*, 2 vols. (trans. Henry Reeve, London, 1835), 2, 232–3.

A NOTE ON THE RESOURCES OF THE LIBRARY OF CONGRESS FOR THE STUDY OF RELIGION IN EARLY AMERICA ✧

All of the world's major religions are extensively documented in the collections of the Library of Congress. Not surprisingly, the religious groups who settled British North America and who survived and prospered in the independent United States are especially well represented in the Library's holdings, as the present exhibit attests.

The Library's General Collections, which contain immense numbers of monographs, journals, and other printed material on religion in early America, are the obvious starting point for any study or exhibit on the subject. Containing, as they do, printed secondary sources, the General Collections furnished far fewer items for this exhibit than did the Library's Special Collections, which hold rich veins of original material, in their respective formats, on religion in general and on religion in early America in particular.

The Rare Book and Special Collections Division is a major repository for the study of early American religious history. It holds the Library's remarkable Bible Collection, containing some 1,470 bibles, dating from the dawn of printing. The division also holds the records of the Virginia Company of London, which document the fortunes of the Church of England in the early decades of the Old Dominion. Thousands of printed sermons, dating from the sixteenth to the early nineteenth century, are contained in the following collections: Miscellaneous Pamphlets, Theological Pamphlets, Peter Force, Ebenezer Hazard, Toner, and American Imprints. An important, though infrequently used, resource for the study of American religion is the extensive Broadside Collection (30,500 items), mostly single sheet publications, containing extensive information about denominational activities and official actions affecting religion in early America. A related collection, the Continental Congress Broadsides, document the Continental-Confederation Congress's extensive actions in the religious sphere. Special collections in the Rare Book Division by no means exhaust the division's resources for the study of religion. Indeed, a substantial portion of the division's holdings through the end of the eighteenth century relate to religion, as the most cursory investigation of its card catalog and databases will reveal.

The Manuscript Division is also a major source for the study of early American religion, although its collections tend to focus more on the public aspect of religion, i.e., church-state relations—than on its more private, denominational dimensions. The reason is that the Manuscript Division holds the major collections of the founders of the American nation—Washington, Jefferson, Madison, Hamilton, and others—and those papers reveal the various approaches taken to the old, vexing problem of adjusting the relations between church and state in the new nation. The division does not lack, however, collections that focus on denominational concerns, especially the transcriptions of the records of the Anglican Society for the Propagation of the Gospel in Foreign Parts (SPG) and of the records at Lambeth Palace, the administrative headquarters of the Church of England.

The Prints and Photographs Division holds a large collection of images, both originals and reproductions, of significant episodes in American religious history, as well as of religious leaders and churches. A particularly valuable resource for the study of early American religion is the Historical American Buildings Survey (HABS) Collection, which contains descriptions, architectural drawings, and photographs of surviving colonial churches.

The resources of the Geography and Map Division for the study of American religion are strongest for the nineteenth and twentieth centuries, for which they contain large numbers of maps showing the geographical distribution of denominations in the United States. The division, however, holds some maps which show the location of churches in the colonial period.

The Music Division has excellent collections of nineteenth-century revival hymnals as well as music performed in American churches in the eighteenth century.

SELECT BIBLIOGRAPHY ♧

Ahlstrom, Sydney, *A Religious History of the American People* (New Haven: Yale University Press, 1972).

Bebbington, David W., *Evangelicalism in Modern Britain* (London: Unwin Hyman, 1989).

Bloch, Ruth H., *Visionary republic: millennial themes in American thought 1756–1800* (Cambridge: Cambridge University Press, 1985).

Boles, John, *The Great Revival, 1787–1805: the origins of the Southern evangelical mind* (Lexington: University Press of Kentucky, 1972).

Bonomi, Patricia, *Under the Cope of Heaven* (New York: Oxford University Press, 1986).

Breen, Timothy, *The Character of the Good Ruler* (New Haven: Yale University Press, 1970).

Buckley, Thomas E., *Church and State in Revolutionary Virginia, 1776–1787* (Charlottesville: University Press of Virginia, 1977).

Bushman, Richard, ed., *The Great Awakening: Documents on the Revival of Religion* (New York: Atheneum, 1970).

Butler, Jon, *Awash in a Sea of Faith: Christianizing the American People* (Cambridge, Massachusetts: Harvard University Press, 1990).

Carwardine, Richard, *Trans-Atlantic Revivalism: Popular Evangelicalism in Britain and America 1790–1815* (Westport, Connecticut: Greenwood Press, 1978).

Cole, Charles, *The Social Ideas of Northern Evangelists* (New York: Octagon Books, 1966).

Cooke, Jacob E., ed., *Encyclopedia of the North American Colonies*, 3 vols. (New York: Charles Scribner's Sons, 1993).

Crawford, Michael J., *Seasons of Grace* (New York: Oxford University Press, 1991).

Curry, Thomas J., *The First Freedoms: Church and State in America to the Passage of the First Amendment* (New York: Oxford University Press, 1986).

Foster, Charles I., *An Errand of Mercy: The Evangelical United Front 1790–1837* (Chapel Hill: University of North Carolina Press, 1960).

Gaustad, Edwin S., *Faith of our Fathers* (San Francisco: Harper & Row, 1987).

Gaustad, Edwin S., *Historical Atlas of Religion in America* (New York: Harper & Row, 1962).

Gaustad, Edwin S., *The Great Awakening in New England* (New York: Harpers, 1957).

Gaustad, Edwin S., *Sworn on the Altar of God: A Religious Biography of Thomas Jefferson* (Grand Rapids, Michigan: William B. Eerdmans Publishing Co., 1996).

Griffin, Clifford, *Their Brothers' Keeper: Moral Stewardship in the United States, 1800–1865* (Westport, Connecticut: Greenwood Press, 1983).

Hall, David, *The Faithful Shepherd* (Chapel Hill: University of North Carolina Press, 1972).

Hatch, Nathan O., *The Democratization of American Christianity* (New Haven: Yale University Press, 1989).

Heimert, Alan, *Religion and the American Mind* (Cambridge, Massachusetts: Harvard University Press, 1966).

Heyrman, Christine Leigh, *Southern Cross: The Beginnings of the Bible Belt* (New York: Alfred A. Knopf, 1997).

Hoffman, Ronald, and Peter Albert, eds., *Religion in a Revolutionary Age* (Charlottesville: University Press of Virginia, 1994).

Hood, Fred J., *Reformed America: The Middle and Southern States 1783–1837* (University, Alabama: University Press of Alabama, 1980).

Juster, Susan, *Disorderly Women: Sexual Politics & Evangelicalism in Revolutionary New England* (Ithaca, New York: Cornell University Press, 1994).

Keller, Charles, *The Second Great Awakening in Connecticut* (Hamden, Connecticut: Anchor Books, 1968).

McLoughlin, William, *Isaac Backus and the American Pietistic Tradition* (Boston: Little, Brown and Company, 1967).

Miller, Perry, *Errand into the Wilderness* (Cambridge, Massachusetts: Harvard University Press, 1956).

Miller, Perry, *Orthodoxy in Massachusetts, 1630–1650* (New York: Harper & Row, 1970).

Miller, Perry, *The New England Mind from Colony to Province* (Cambridge, Massachusetts: Harvard University Press, 1953).

Noll, Mark, *Christians in the American Revolution* (Grand Rapids, Michigan: Christian University Press, 1977).

Noll, Mark, David W. Bebbington, George A. Rawlyk, eds., *Evangelicalism* (New York: Oxford University Press, 1994).

Noll, Mark, ed., *Religion and American Politics* (New York: Oxford University Press, 1990).

Rahe, Paul A., *Republics Ancient and Modern* (Chapel Hill: University of North Carolina Press, 1992).

Schmidt, Leigh Eric, *Holy fairs: Scottish communions and American revivals in the early modern period* (Princeton, New Jersey: Princeton University Press, 1989).

Smylie, James, *American Presbyterians: A Pictorial History* (Philadelphia: Presbyterian Historical Society, 1985).

Stout, Harry, *The New England Soul: preaching and religious culture in colonial New England* (New York: Oxford University Press, 1986).

Tweed, Thomas A., ed., *Retelling U.S. religious history* (Berkeley: University of California Press, 1997).

West, John G., Jr., *The Politics of Revelation and Reason* (Lawrence: University Press of Kansas, 1996).

Westerkamp, Marilyn, *The Triumph of the Laity: Scots-Irish Piety and the Great Awakening, 1625–1760* (New York: Oxford University Press, 1988).

CATALOGUE OF OBJECTS IN THE EXHIBITION

AMERICA AS A RELIGIOUS REFUGE: THE SEVENTEENTH CENTURY

■ Murder of David van der Leyen and Levina Ghyselins, Ghent, 1554. Engraving by J. Luyken, in T. J. V. Bracht (or Thieleman van Braght), *Het Bloedig Touneel De Martelaers Spiegel. . . .* (Amsterdam, 1685). Library of Congress (LC), Rare Book and Special Collections Division (RBSCD). (LC-USZ62-119890) (*p. 2*).

■ Mass murder of Huguenots, 1562. Lithograph in A. Challe, *Histoire des Guerres du Calvinisme et de la ligue dans l'auxerrois, le sénonais et les autres contrées qui forment aujourd'hui le département de L'yonne* (Auxerre, 1863). LC, General Collections (GC).

■ Huguenots, as persecutors of Catholics. Engraving in Richard Verstegen, *Théâtre des Cruautez des Hérétiques de notre temps* (Antwerp, 1607). Folger Shakespeare Library, Washington, D.C.

■ Execution and mutilation of John Ogilvie (Ogilby), S.J., Glasgow, Scotland, March 10, 1615. Engraving in Mathias Tanner, *Societas Jesu usque ad sanguinis et vitae profusionem Militans. . . .* (Prague, 1675). LC, RBSCD (LC-USZ62-119891) (*p. 4*).

■ Protestants killed by Irish Catholics, 1641, in Matthew Taylor, *England's Bloody Tribunal. . . .* (London, 1773). LC, RBSCD.

■ Jesuits persecuted in England, 1643–4, in Mathias Tanner, *Die Gesellshafft Jesu biss zur vergiessung ihres Blutes. . . .* (Prague, 1683). LC, RBSCD.

■ Expulsion of the Salzburgers, 1731 (*Die Freundliche Bewillkommung . . .*). Engraving by David Böecklin (Leipzig, 1732). New York Public Library.

■ Lutheran religious refugees fleeing Salzburg, Austria. Frontispiece engraving in [Christopher Sancke?], *Ausführliche Historie derer Emigranten oder Vertriebenen Lutheraner aus dem Erz-Bistum Salzburg* (Leipzig, 1732). Reformation Collection, LC, RBSCD (LC-USZ62-119892) (*p. 5*).

■ The burning of Master John Rogers. . . . in John Fox, *The Third Volume of the Ecclesiastical History containing the Acts and Monuments of Martyrs. . . .* (London, 1684). LC, RBSCD.

■ The burning of Mr. John Rogers in *The New England Primer Improved* (Boston, 1773). LC, RBSCD.

■ Richard Mather, copyprint of relief cut by John Foster, ca. 1670. American Antiquarian Society, Worcester, Massachusetts.

■ *Cottonus Matherus* [Cotton Mather], 1727. Mezzotint by Peter Pelham, 1728 (Restrike, 1860). LC, Prints & Photographs Division (P&P) (LC-USZC4-4597) (*p. 6*).

■ Cotton Mather, draft fragments of a sermon. Miscellaneous Manuscript Collection, LC, Manuscript Division (MSS) (*p. 6*).

■ *The Bible and Holy Scriptures Conteyned in the Olde and Newe Testament. Translated according to the Ebrue and Greke, and conferred with the best translations in divers languages. . . .* (Geneva, 1560). Bible Collection, LC, RBSCD.

■ *The Holy Bible Conteyning the Old Testament and the New* (King James Bible), (London, 1611). LC, RBSCD.

■ *The General Laws and Liberties of the Massachusetts Colony: Revised and Reprinted* (Cambridge, Massachusetts, 1672). LC, Law Library, Rare Book Collection.

■ *The Whole Booke of Psalmes Faithfully Translated into English Metre* (The Bay Psalm Book). (Cambridge, Massachusetts, 1640). LC, RBSCD.

■ *The Holy Bible Containing the Old Testaments, translated into the Indian Language* (the "Eliot Bible") (Cambridge, Massachusetts, 1663). LC, RBSCD.

■ Roger Williams, *The Bloody Tenent of Persecution, for cause of Conscience, discussed in a Conference between Truth and Peace. . . .* (1644). LC, RBSCD.

- Mary Dyer led to execution. Copyprint of an etching. The Granger Collection, New York.

- Thomas Jefferson, *Notes on the State of Virginia* (New York, 1801). LC, RBSCD.

- Touro Synagogue, Newport, Rhode Island. Copyprint of photograph by Jack Boucher, 1971. Historic American Buildings Survey, LC, P&P.

- Sefardi Torah scroll, eighteenth century (?). LC, Hebraic Section, African and Middle Eastern Division (*p. 9*).

- German breastplate, c.1810. Touro Synagogue, Newport, Rhode Island.

- Matza board, eighteenth century. Touro Synagogue, Newport, Rhode Island.

- William Penn, age 22. Eighteenth-century copy of a lost original portrait, possibly by Sir Peter Lely, 1666. Historical Society of Pennsylvania.

- William Penn, *The Frame of government of the province of Pennsilvania in America* (1682). LC, RBSCD.

- The Quaker Meeting, c.1677. Engraving by Marcel Lauron, after a painting by Egbert van Heemskerk. Haverford College, Haverford, Pennsylvania.

- *A Collection of Christian & Brotherly Advices.* . . . (Quaker Book of Discipline, c.1763). Miscellaneous Manuscripts Collections, LC, MSS.

- William Penn, *Missive van William Penn . . . Geschreven aan de Commissarissen van de vrye Societeyt der Handelaars* (Amsterdam, 1684). LC, RBSCD.

- Pennsylvania German baptismal certificate, 1807. German Fraktur Collection, LC, P&P.

- *Das neue Jerusalem.* Woodcut with watercolor, artist unidentified, early nineteenth century. German Fraktur Collection, LC, P&P (LC-USZC4-4570) (*p. 14*).

- *Pedilavium das Füsswaschen der Schwestern.* Engraving from David Cranz, *Kurze, Zuverlässige Nachricht, von der, unter den*

Namen der Böhmisch-Mährischen Brüder Bekannt, Kirche Unitas fratrum (Halle, 1757). The Library Company of Philadelphia (*p. 13*).

- Father Andrew White. Engraving in Mathias Tanner, *Societas Jesu apostolorum imitatrix* (Prague, 1694). Special Collections Division, Georgetown University Library.

- Father Andrew White, prayers in the Piscataway Indian language. Special Collections Division, Georgetown University Library.

- Maryland Act Concerning Religion, 1649. Maryland State Archives, Annapolis.

- Cecil Calvert presenting to Lycurgus his "Act Concerning Religion," 1649. Engraving by James Barry, 1793. LC, P&P (*p. 16*).

- Catholic Church at St. Mary's City, Maryland, c.1670. Copyprint of twentieth-century rendering. Historic St. Mary's City.

- Catholic artifacts, seventeenth century; Georgetown University (ostensorium) and Historic St. Mary's City (medals and clay figurine).

- *The Book of Common-Prayer and Administration of the Sacraments, and other Rites and Ceremonies of the Church, According to the Use of the Church of England.* . . . (London, 1662). LC, RBSCD.

- Morning Prayer. The Apostles Creed. The Lords Prayer. The Second Collect, for Peace, from *The Book of Common Prayer in Short-Hand, According to Mr. Weston's Excellent Method.* . . . (London, 1730). LC, RBSCD (*p. 17*).

- Virginia Company of London, Instructions to Gov. George Yeardley, November 18, 1618. Virginia Miscellaneous Records, 1606–1692 (the Bland Manuscript), Jefferson Collection, LC, RBSCD.

- The Baptism of Pocahontas. Oil study by John Gadsby Chapman, c.1837–40. Jamestown-Yorktown Foundation.

- Communion silver used at Jamestown, c.1661. The Trustees and Vestry of Bruton Parish Church, Williamsburg.

- Ordination papers of Reverend Thomas Read from the Church of England, with carrying case, 1773. Washington National Cathedral.

RELIGION IN EIGHTEENTH-CENTURY AMERICA

- *Nieuw Amsterdam* (New York City), c.1651–55. Copyprint of detail from *Novi Belgi* (Amsterdam, c.1690). Hand-colored engraved map. LC, Geography & Map Division (G&M).

- *A View of Fort George with City of New York from the SW*, c.1730. Engraving by I. Carwitham. LC, P&P (LC-USZ62-19360).

- View of New York City, 1771. Copyprint of woodcut from Hugh Gaine, *New York Almanac*, 1771. American Antiquarian Society, Worcester, Massachusetts.

- St. James Church, Goose Creek, S.C. (exterior). Photograph by Frances Benjamin Johnston. LC, P&P (LC-J7-SC-1476).

- St. James Church, Goose Creek, S.C. (interior). Photograph by Frances Benjamin Johnston. LC, P&P (LC-J7-SC-1479A).

- Christ Church, Philadelphia, 1787. Engraving in *Columbian Magazine*, September 1786–December 1787. LC, RBSCD.

- South Quay Baptist Church (exterior). Copyprint of photograph. Virginia Baptist Historical Society (*p. 20*).

- Mt. Shiloh Baptist Church (interior). Copyprint of photograph. Virginia Baptist Historical Society.

- *A SW View of the Baptist Meeting House, Providence, R.I.* Engraving by S. Hill for *Massachusetts Magazine*, August 1789. LC, RBSCD (LC-USZ62-31789) (*p. 20*).

■ *In Side the Old Lutheran Church in 1800, York, Pa.* Watercolor with pen and ink by Lewis Miller. Historical Society of York County, York, Pennsylvania (*p. 23*).

■ John Locke, *Letters Concerning Toleration* (London, 1765). LC, RBSCD.

■ John Toland, *Christianity Not Mysterious* (London, 1696). LC, RBSCD (*p. 25*).

■ *The Philosophical Works of the late Right Honourable Henry St. John, Lord Viscount Bolingbroke,* Vol. 2 (London, 1754). LC, RBSCD.

■ Thomas Jefferson, Literary Commonplace Book. Jefferson Papers, LC, MSS.

■ George Whitefield. Oil painting attributed to Joseph Badger, c.1743–65. Harvard University.

■ George Whitefield's field pulpit. American Tract Society, Garland, Texas (*p. 28*).

■ George Whitefield, *Marks of the New Birth* (New York, 1739). American Imprints, LC, RBSCD.

■ *Dr. Squintum's Exaltation or the Reformation.* Engraving, London, 1763. LC, P&P (LC-USZ62-108225).

■ George Whitefield burial scene. Woodcut in Phillis Wheatley, *Poem by Phillis, a Negro Girl, in Boston. On the Death of the Reverend George Whitefield* (Boston, 1770). American Imprints, LC, RBSCD (*p. 28*).

■ Jonathan Edwards. Carved wooden bust by Keith Wilbur, 1982.

■ Jonathan Edwards, *A Faithful Narrative of the Surprising Work of God. . . .* (London, 1737). LC, RBSCD.

■ Jonathan Edwards, *Sinners in the Hands of an Angry God* (Boston, 1741). New York Public Library.

■ John Wesley, *The Distinguishing Marks of a Work of the Spirit of God, Extracted from Mr. Edwards* (London, 1744). LC, RBSCD (*p. 26*).

■ Gilbert Tennent. Oil on canvas, attributed to Gustavus Hesselius, undated. Princeton University.

■ Gilbert Tennent, *The Danger of an Unconverted Ministry* (Philadelphia, 1740). American Imprints, LC, RBSCD.

■ Samuel Blair, *An Account of the College of New Jersey* (Woodbridge, 1764). LC, RBSCD.

■ Samuel Davies. Portrait. Artist and date unknown. Union Theological Seminary, Richmond, Virginia.

■ Presbyterian communion tokens. Courtesy of Martha Hopkins.

■ Baptism in Schuylkill River. Photograph of woodcut from Morgan Edwards, *Materials Towards A History of the American Baptists* (Philadelphia, 1770). Historical Society of Pennsylvania (*p. 31*).

■ Views of Jones Falls, Baltimore, September 13, 1818. Engraving. Maryland Historical Society, Baltimore.

■ Francis Asbury. Oil painting by Charles Peale Polk, 1794. Lovely Lane Museum of United Methodist Historical Society, Baltimore (*p. 32*).

■ *The Rigging House,* site of first Methodist services in New York City, 1766. Color lithograph by A. R. Robinson, 1846. LC, P&P (LC-USZ62-16819).

■ G. Stebbins and G. King, *Methodist Itinerant System.* Broadside, New York, 1810–11 [?]. Rare Book Division, New York Public Library (*p. 34*).

RELIGION AND THE AMERICAN REVOLUTION

■ Joseph Galloway, *Historical and Political Reflections on the Rise and Progress of the American Rebellion* (London, 1780). LC, RBSCD.

■ *Jonathan Mayhew, D.D. Pastor of the West Church in Boston.* Etching by Giovanni Cipriani, London, 1767. American Antiquarian Society, Worcester, Massachusetts (*p. 39*).

■ *Antisejanus. Drink deep, or taste not the Porterial Spring.* Etching [1765]. P&P (LC-USZ6Z-45398) (*p. 40*).

■ Jonathan Mayhew, *Discourse Concerning Unlimited Submission and Non-Resistance to the Higher Powers* (Boston, 1750). LC, RBSCD.

■ The Hanging of Absalom. Needlework (silk and metal thread on black satin, with painted details) by Faith Robinson Trumbull, c.1770. Lyman Allyn Art Museum, New London, Connecticut (*cover and p. 36*).

■ *An Attempt to Land a Bishop in America.* Engraving from the

Political Register, London, September 1769. John Carter Brown Library, Providence, Rhode Island (*p. 41*).

■ Abraham Keteltas, *God arising and pleading his People's Cause, or the American War . . . shewn to be the Cause of God* (Newburyport, Massachusetts, 1777). American Imprints, LC, RBSCD (*p. 43*).

■ *The Yankie Doodles Intrenchments Near Boston 1776.* Copyprint of etching. British Museum (*p. 42*).

■ John Peter Gabriel Muhlenberg. Oil on canvas by an unidentified American artist, nineteenth century. Martin Art Gallery, Muhlenberg College, Allentown, Pennsylvania (*p. 44*).

■ *Reverend James Caldwell at the Battle of Springfield.* Oil painting by Henry Alexander Ogden. Undated. Presbyterian Historical Society, Philadelphia (*p. 45*).

■ Gostelowe Standard No. 10, Armed Resistance. Photograph

of a watercolor once in the possession of Edward W. Richardson. Courtesy of Pennsylvania Society of Sons of the Revolution and Its Color Guard, Philadelphia (*p. 43*).

■ John Witherspoon. Oil painting by Charles Willson Peale. National Portrait Gallery, Smithsonian Institution (LC-USZ6Z-10022). (*p. 46*).

■ Free Quaker Meeting House. Photograph. Carson Collection, LC, MSS.

■ *To those of our Brethren who have disowned us.* Free Quaker broadside, 1781. Carson Collection, LC, MSS.

■ Books of Common Prayer, altered to remove prayers for the King of England. Washington National Cathedral and Christ Church, Philadelphia.

■ Jonathan Odell, *The Times, A Satirical Poem* (printed but not published, 1780). LC, RBSCD.

■ William White, *The Case of the Episcopal Churches in the United States Considered* (Philadelphia, 1782). LC, RBSCD.

■ *The Ordination of Bishop Asbury, Dec. 27th, 1784.* Engraving, after a painting by Thomas Coke Ruckle, 1882. Lovely Lane Museum of United Methodist Historical Society, Baltimore.

■ *Acts and Proceedings of the Synod of New-York and Philadelphia, A.D. 1787, & 1788* (Philadelphia, 1788). American Imprints, LC, RBSCD.

RELIGION AND THE CONGRESS OF THE CONFEDERATION, 1776-1789

■ Jacob Duché offering the first prayer in Congress, September 7, 1774. The Liberty Window, Christ Church, Philadelphia, after a painting by Harrison Tompkins Matteson, c.1848. Christ Church, Philadelphia (*p. 48*).

■ Congressional resolution to pay chaplains, April 22, 1782. Continental Congress Broadsides, LC, RBSCD.

■ George Duffield. Oil on canvas by Charles Peale Polk, 1790. Independence National Historical Park, Philadelphia.

■ Benjamin Franklin, legend for great seal of the United States, 1776. Jefferson Papers, LC, MSS (LCMS-27748-181) (*p. 50*).

■ Thomas Jefferson, legend for great seal of the United States, 1776. Jefferson Papers, LC, MSS (LCMS-27748-182) (*p. 50*).

■ Proposed great seal of the United States, "Rebellion to Tyrants is Obedience to God." Drawing by Benson J. Lossing, 1856, published in Richard S. Patterson and Richardson Dougall, *The Eagle and the Shield* (Washington, D.C., 1976). Reference Collection, LC, MSS (*p. 51*).

■ Congressional fast day proclamation, March 16, 1776. Broadside Collection, LC, RBSCD (*p. 52*).

■ Congressional thanksgiving proclamation, November 1, 1777. Broadside Collection, LC, RBSCD.

■ Congressional fast day proclamation, March 20, 1779. Continental Congress Broadsides, LC, RBSCD.

■ Congressional thanksgiving proclamation, October 11, 1782. Continental Congress Broadsides, LC, RBSCD.

■ Continental Army, Rules and Regulations, November 1775. American Imprints, LC, RBSCD.

■ *To all brave, healthy, able bodied well disposed young men. . . .* Recruiting poster for the Continental Army, 1798. Historical Society of Pennsylvania.

■ Continental Navy, Rules and Regulations, November 1775. American Imprints, LC, RBSCD.

■ Horn beaker with scrimshaw portrait of Esek Hopkins. Mariner's Museum, Newport News, Virginia.

■ Congressional resolution, September 12, 1782, endorsing the Aitken Bible, in *Journals of Congress*, September, 1782. LC, RBSCD (*p. 55*).

■ *The Holy Bible Containing the Old and New Testaments Newly translated out of the Original Tongues. . . .* (Robert Aitken's Bible) (Philadelphia, 1782). LC, RBSCD (*p. 56*).

■ Land Ordinance of 1785. Continental Congress Broadsides, LC, RBSCD.

■ Northwest Ordinance of 1787. Continental Congress Broadsides, LC, RBSCD.

■ Congressional resolution, July 27, 1787, alloting lands for christianizing the Delaware Indians. National Archives and Records Administration.

■ David Zeisberger, *Delaware Indian and English Spelling Book* (Philadelphia, 1806). LC, RBSCD.

RELIGION AND THE STATE GOVERNMENTS, 1776-1787

■ John Jewel, *A Defense of the Apologie of the Church of England* (London, 1570). LC, RBSCD.

■ *The Humble Advice of the Assembly of Divines by Authority of Parliament sitting at Westminster; Concerning a Confession of Faith* (London, 1658). LC, RBSCD.

■ Edward Dorr, *The Duty of Civil Rulers, to be Nursing Fathers to the Church of Christ* (Hartford, Connecticut, 1765). American Imprints, LC, RBSCD (*p. 60*).

■ Massachusetts fast day proclamation, April 15, 1775. Broadside Collection, LC, RBSCD.

- Amherst County, Virginia, petition to Virginia Assembly, November 27, 1783. Library of Virginia, Richmond.

- Phillips Payson, *Election Sermon*, May 27, 1778. American Imprints, LC, RBSCD.

- Isaac Backus, *Government and Liberty Described and Ecclesiastical Tyranny Exposed* (Boston, 1778). John Carter Brown Library, Providence, Rhode Island.

- *Rev. Isaac Backus, AM*. Oil on canvas by unidentified artist undated. Trask Library, Andover-Newton Theological School, Newton Centre, Massachusetts (*p. 69*).

- "Irenaeus," *The Boston Gazette and the Country Journal*, November 27, 1780. LC, Serial and Government Publications Division.

- *A Declaration of the Rights of the Inhabitants of the Commonwealth of Massachusetts* [Massachusetts Constitution or Frame of Government, 1780]. American Imprints, LC, RBSCD (*p. 63*).

- [Maryland] House of Delegates, *An Act to lay a general tax for the support of the ministers of the gospel . . .* , January 12, 1785. Broadside Collection, LC, RBSCD (*p. 64*).

- George Mason, Virginia Bill of Rights, May 1776. LC, MSS.

- [Patrick Henry], *A Bill Establishing a Provision for Teachers of the Christian Religion*, [Virginia] House of Delegates, December 24, 1784. Broadside. Washington Papers, LC, MSS (LCMS-44693-177) (*p. 66*).

- Patrick Henry. Copyprint of stipple engraving by Leney, after Thomas Sully, 1817. LC, P&P (LC-USZ62-4907) (*p. 67*).

- James Madison. Miniature painting by Charles Willson Peale, 1783. LC, RBSCD (LC-USZC4-5310) (*p. 67*).

- John Marshall. Medallion engraving by Charles Balthazar Julien Fevret de Saint-Memin, 1808. LC, P&P (LC-USZ62-54940) (*p. 67*).

- George Washington, letter to George Mason, October 3, 1785. Washington Papers, LC, MSS.

- Surry County, Virginia, petition to Virginia Assembly, November 14, 1785. Library of Virginia, Richmond.

- Westmoreland County, Virginia, petition to Virginia Assembly, November 2, 1785. Library of Virginia, Richmond.

- Warrant for arrest of Nathaniel Saunders, Virginia Baptist minister, for unlawful preaching. Virginia Baptist Historical Society, Richmond.

- The dunking of David Barrow and Edward Mintz in the Nansemond River, 1778. Oil painting by Sidney E. King, 1990. Virginia Baptist Historical Society, Richmond (*p. 71*).

- James Madison, *A Memorial and Remonstrance*, [June 1785]. LC, MSS (LCMS-31021-86) (*p. 72*).

- Richard Henry Lee, letter to James Madison, November 26, 1784. Madison Papers, LC, MSS.

- Thomas Jefferson, *An Act for Establishing Religious Freedom*, January 1786. Broadside Collection, LC, RBSCD (*p. 73*).

RELIGION AND THE FEDERAL GOVERNMENT

- Benjamin Franklin, speech, Constitutional Convention, June 28, 1787. Franklin Papers, LC, MSS.

- Article 6, Constitution of the United States (William Jackson copy). LC, MSS.

- Amendments to the Constitution proposed by the Virginia Convention, June 27, 1788. Constitutional Convention broadsides, LC, RBSCD.

- John Leland, Objections to the Federal Constitution, [February 1788]. Madison Papers, LC, MSS.

- James Madison, manuscript outline of speech introducing the Bill of Rights, June 8, 1789. Madison Papers, LC, MSS.

- Bill of Rights, official copy on vellum, as sent to the states, September 1789. LC, RBSCD.

- George Washington. Chalk drawing on paper, c.1800, by Charles Balthazar Julien Fevret de Saint-Memin. LC, P&P.

- George Washington, Truro Parish Vestry Book, June 5, 1772. LC, MSS.

- George Washington, circular to the chief executives of the states, June 11, 1783. Washington Papers, LC, MSS (LCMS-44693-176) (*p. 76*).

- George Washington, letter to the Touro Synagogue, August 17, 1790. Washington Papers, LC, MSS.

- Alexander Hamilton, draft of Washington's Farewell Address, [July] 1796. Hamilton Papers, LC, MSS.

- George Washington, *The Address of Gen. Washington to the People of America on his Declining the Presidency of the United States* (Farewell Address), September 19, 1796. Broadside Collection, LC, RBSCD.

- John Adams, letter to Thomas Jefferson, April 19, 1817. Jefferson Papers, LC, MSS.

- John Adams, fast day proclamation, March 23, 1798. Broadside Collection, LC, RBSCD.

- *The Providential Detection*. Cartoon etching by an anonymous artist, 1800. The Library Company of Philadelphia (*p. 81*).

- Thomas Jefferson, letter to Benjamin Rush, April 21, 1803 (with "syllabus" on the doctrines of Jesus). Jefferson Papers, LC, MSS.

- The Lord's Prayer, in Thomas Jefferson's hand. Jefferson Papers, LC, MSS (LCMS-27748-276) (*p. 82*).

- The "Jefferson Bible" (The Life and Morals of Jesus of Nazareth Extracted textually from the Gospels in Greek, Latin, French & English). National Museum of American History, Smithsonian Institution.

- Thomas Jefferson, To Messrs. Nehemiah Dodge, Ephraim Robbins, & Stephen S. Nelson a committee of the Danbury Baptist Association in the state of Connecticut, January 1, 1802. Jefferson Papers, LC, MSS (LCMS-27748-36A and B) (p. 85).

- Manasseh Cutler, diary, January 3, 1802. McCormick Library of Special Collections, Northwestern University Library (p. 87).

- Manasseh Cutler, letter to Joseph Torrey, January 3, 1803. McCormick Library of Special Collections, Northwestern University Library.

- Margaret Bayard Smith, Reminiscences, 1828. Margaret B. Smith Papers, LC, MSS.

- Catharine Akerly Mitchill, letter to her sister Margaret Miller, April 8, 1806. Catharine A. Mitchill Papers, LC, MSS (LCMS-34819-3) (p. 90).

- Abijah Bigelow, letter to Hannah Bigelow, December 28, 1812. American Antiquarian Society, Worcester, Massachusetts (p. 95).

- Members of the United States Marine Corps Band, c.1798. Copyprint of original art by Lt. Col. Donna Neary, USMCR. "The President's Own" United States Marine Corps Band (p. 89).

- *The Old House of Representatives.* Copyprint of oil painting by Samuel F. B. Morse, 1822. The Corcoran Gallery of Art, Washington, D.C. Museum Purchase, Gallery Fund (p. 88).

REPUBLICAN RELIGION

- Thomas Paine, *The Age of Reason* (Philadelphia, 1794). American Imprints, LC, RBSCD.

- *Tom Paine's Nightly Pest.* Aquatint by James Gillray, London, 1792. LC, P&P (LC-USZ62-1550).

- *The Tree of Life.* Hand-colored engraving, Baltimore, 1791. Maryland Historical Society, Baltimore (p. ii).

- *Sacramental Scene in a Western Forest.* Lithograph by P. S. Duval, c.1801, from Joseph Smith, *Old Redstone* (Philadelphia, 1854). LC, GC (LC-USZ62-61152) (p. 101).

- *Plan of the camp,* 1809. Sketch by Benjamin H. Latrobe. Maryland Historical Society, Baltimore.

- *Camp Meeting of the Methodists in America.* Aquatint etching with watercolor by M. Dubourg after J. Milbert, March 1819. LC, P&P (LC-USZC4-772 and LC-USZ62-2497).

- *Religious Camp Meeting.* Watercolor by J. Maze Burbank, c.1839. Old Dartmouth Historical Society-New Bedford Whaling Museum, New Bedford, Massachusetts, Gift of William Havemeyer (p. 102).

- John Hargrove, *A Sermon on the Second Coming of Christ. . . . ,* December 25, 1804. Jefferson Collection, LC, RBSCD.

- John England, *The substance of a discourse preached in the hall of the House of Representatives, January 8, 1826* (Baltimore, 1826). LC, RBSCD.

- Bishop John England. Oil painting. Artist and date unknown. Diocese of Charleston, Charleston, South Carolina.

- *Harriet Livermore.* Engraving by J. B. Longacre, from a painting by Waldo and Jewett, 1827. National Portrait Gallery, Smithsonian Institution (p. 86).

- Manasseh Cutler, diary, December 23, 1804. McCormick Library of Special Collections, Northwestern University Library (p. 90).

- *Washington City.* Watercolor sketch by Baroness Hyde de Neuville, 1820. New York Public Library (p. 94).

- John Quincy Adams, diary, February 2, 1806. Copyprint. Adams Family Papers, Massachusetts Historical Society, Boston (p. 90).

- The Old Supreme Court Chamber, c.1810, U.S. Capitol Building. Copyprint of photograph by Franz Jantzen, Collection of the Supreme Court of the United States (p. 92).

- Charles B. Boynton, fund-raising brochure, Washington, D.C., November 1, 1867. Broadside Collection, LC, RBSCD (p. 91).

- *The House of Representatives, 1866.* Lithograph by E. Sachse & Co. LC, P&P (LC-USZC4-422).

- William Little and William Smith, *The Easy Instructor; or, A New Method of Teaching Sacred Harmony* (Albany, [1798?]); Samuel Wakefield, *The Christian's Harp* (Pittsburgh, 1837). Revival hymnals. LC, Music Division.

- *Bishops of the A.M.E. Church.* Engraving by John H. W. Burley, Washington, D.C., 1876. LC, P&P (LC-USZ62-15059) (p. 104).

- *Mrs. Juliann Jane Tillman, Preacher of the AME Church.* Engraving by P. S. Duval, after a painting by Alfred Hoffy, Philadelphia, 1844. LC, P&P (LC-USZ62-54596) (p. 107).

- Letter from Mt. Pisgah Baptist Church, Rankin City, Mississippi, to Upper King and Queen Baptist Church, Newtown, Virginia, June 1837, concerning the faith and charity of a black female slave, sold away from her family into Mississippi. Virginia Baptist Historical Society, Richmond.

- Absalom Jones. Oil on canvas, mounted on board by Raphaelle Peale, 1810. Delaware Art Museum, Wilmington.

- *Negro Methodists holding a Meeting in Philadelphia*. Watercolor by Pavel (Paul) Petrovich Svinin, c.1811–13. Metropolitan Museum of Art, New York.

- *The Jerking Exercise*. Copyprint of engraving by Lossing-Barritt, c.1840. LC, P&P. (LC-USZ62-38407).

- *Shakers near Lebanon state of N York, their mode of worship*. Stipple and line engraving, drawn from life. LC, P&P. (LC-USZ62-13659) (*p. 108*).

- *Pioneers in the Great Religious Reformation of the Nineteenth Century* (includes Barton Stone and Alexander Campbell). Engraving by J.C. Buttre, after drawing by J.D.C. McFarland, 1885. LC, P&P.

- *The Book of Mormon* (Palmyra, 1830). LC, RBSCD.

- *Martyrdom of Joseph and Hiram Smith in Carthage Jail, June 27, 1844*. Tinted lithograph by Nagel & Weingartner, after C. G. Crehen, New York, 1851. LC, P&P (LC-USZ62-765 and LC-USZC4-4562) (*p. 110*).

- *Route of Mormon Pioneers from Nauvoo to Great Salt Lake, Feb'y 1846–July 1847*. Map, 1899. LC, G&M.

- Family handing out tracts. Title page woodcut by Anderson in *The American Tract Magazine*, August 1825. American Tract Society, Garland, Texas (*p. 111*).

- American Tract Society, religious tracts. YA Pamphlet Collection, LC, RBSCD.

- *The Floating Church of Our Saviour. For Seamen. Built New York Feb. 15th, 1844. . . .* Copyprint of steel engraving. LC, P&P (LC-USZ61-1258) (*p. 112*).

- *The Surveyed Part of Wisconsin*. Lithograph in *The Home Missionary*, November 1839, Vol. XII. LC, GC.

- *Missionary Table, Seventeenth Report, 1843*. American Home Missionary Society pamphlet. American Home Missionary Society Papers, LC, MSS (LCMS-59030-1) (*p. 113*).

- *The Circuit Preacher*. Copyprint of wood engraving, after drawing by Alfred R. Waud. *Harper's Weekly*, October 12, 1867. LC, P&P (LC-USZ62-2670).

- Circuit preacher's saddle bags used by Reverend Samuel E. Alford, c. 1872–89. Lovely Lane Museum of United Methodist Historical Society, Baltimore.

- Alexis de Tocqueville, *Democracy in America*. Translated by Henry Reeve (London, 1835). LC, RBSCD (*p. 114*).

- Millennial Time Line, predicting good times after 1800. Engraving by Amos Doolittle, New Haven, 1806. LC, RBSCD.

INDEX ✂

Page numbers in *italics* refer to illustrations